GRANTS
FOR
NONPROFIT
ORGANIZATIONS

GRANTS
FOR
NONPROFIT
ORGANIZATIONS

A Guide to
Funding and Grant Writing

ELEANOR GILPATRICK

PRAEGER

Westport, Connecticut
London

Library of Congress Cataloging-in-Publication Data

Gilpatrick, Eleanor G.
    Grants for nonprofit organizations : a guide to funding and grant
writing / Eleanor Gilpatrick.
            p.   cm.
    Bibliography: p.
    ISBN 0-275-93274-5 (alk. paper)
    1. Fund raising. 2. Research grants. 3. Proposal writing in
research. 4. Corporations, Nonprofit—Finance. I. Title.
HG177.G56   1989
658.1'5224—dc19   88-36978

Library of Congress Catalog Card Number: 88-36978
ISBN: 0-275-93274-5

First published in 1989

Praeger Publishers, 88 Post Road West, Westport, CT 06881
An imprint of Greenwood Publishing Group, Inc.

Printed in the United States of America

The paper used in this book complies with the Permanent
Paper Standard issued by the National Information Standards
Organization (Z39.48--1984).

10 9 8 7 6 5

Contents

Illustrations

EXHIBITS

FIGURES

TABLES

Acknowledgments

Several people helped make this book a reality: first, Dr. Essie Lee, who kept telling me to write handouts for the course; second, the students, who taught me what to write about through their own work; and third, the fine editorial feedback and suggestions I received from Charles G. Arthur; Dr. Annette Ramirez de Arellano, Associate Dean of the School of Health Sciences; Judith A. Harvey; and David Grant.

Special thanks go to the following colleagues and students for their grant proposal ideas and material: Iris Harvell, Richard Marsella, Dr. Beth Richie, and Jade Singer.

Thank you all.

Introduction

This book is designed for the professional in an organization who has the responsibility of preparing grant proposals, and for other individuals who expect to do so someday. It can also be used in a course on grant writing, but is designed to be used alone.

I felt the need to write this book after ten years of successful funding, when I returned to teaching and was asked to teach a course in grant writing. Having scoured the literature in the field, I found an absence of a consistent, intellectual/taxonomic structure and an absence of detailed "how to" steps. Inadequate attention was given to program planning and to the evaluation section in grant proposals.

The book draws from and builds on the field of program evaluation and on the pioneering work of Norton J. Kiritz, executive director of the Grantsmanship Center in Los Angeles. It provides a conceptual taxonomy that can distinguish among a project's problems, methods, objectives, and evaluation design and shows the interrelationships among them.

One of the more helpful parts of the book should be the frequent use of examples based on real situations to take the reader through the steps of the process and show what applications of the ideas might look like. Included are steps in finding funding sources and a set of cumulative writing steps that build toward the final proposal.

1

Overview, Terminology, and Getting Started

OVERVIEW

This book is a step-by-step guide to take you through all the activities and processes you would be expected to carry out in getting funding for a program, from the first idea, to finding a funding source, to the final proposal, and beyond. It is about grant writing, but you will find that it is also about program planning and working within an organization.

The book assumes that an organization is seeking funds. Grants for individuals are rare. The principles are similar, but for an institution you have to deal with all the administration and staff in the various departments involved with the project, while at the same time considering yourself. *You* are important because the presence or absence of enthusiasm in the grant writer is quite apparent in the writing and will affect the results.

The book assumes that you or your employer wants you to write a grant proposal now or in the future. You may have a specific grant idea and granting agency in mind, or you may be assigned to developing grant proposals with no immediate proposal in mind at the time. The book is designed for all these cases.

The book is arranged in chapters, some of which are writing steps that build toward the final proposal. Writing is a skill, and the writing is designed to give you cumulative practice. Try to actually do the writing as you follow the steps to getting funded.

TERMINOLOGY

This book uses terms for specific aspects of grant development that are also in common, everyday use. So it pays to see the specific meanings they will carry.

The *program* is the service or activity for which your organization is trying to get funding. Your agency already runs programs that deliver services. The *funding agency* also has programs, which are the planned objectives for which they offer funding to *applicant agencies*. Therefore the term *project* is more precise; it implies a finite funding period after which the project's program can continue within your agency. In practice, however, the terms *program* and *project* are used as synonyms.

The people to benefit from your proposal, and specifically the ones you hope to work with during the project period, are often called the *target population*.

A *proposal* is a written description of the activity, purpose, expected results, and budget for a project and is usually required whenever grant or contract funds are allocated competitively. But a proposal is not a sales pitch.

The granting agency will evaluate your proposal for funding in terms of the relevance of your ideas to its own aims, the significance of the problem you are addressing, the power of your suggested solution compared with other attempts, the wider effects, the probability of your success, the degree to which you can provide proof of your success, and the clarity with which you present your case.

The proposal is often the only point of communication with a funding agency's decision makers. So it is worth investing the time and effort to make a persuasive, clear case.

The term *grant,* when used narrowly, means funding for unsolicited proposals, but the term is also used more broadly to cover projects funded as *contracts*. Contracts have more restrictions than grants, particularly with respect to accountability, and they are reimbursed after costs are incurred; grants get the funding up front.

Programs go through developmental stages, and these give rise to *types of projects*. Table 1.1 presents a schematic arrangement of the stages through which a program idea may go. These include developmental stages such as planning, mounting a feasibility study to see if the idea can actually work in practice, a demonstration to show how it does work, and the initial experience with implementation. Then comes the operations phase, Number II in Table 1.1, which means the regular day-to-day presentation of the service — for which funding is generally

TABLE 1.1
Stages of Program Development

Stage	Purpose	Type of Project
I. DEVELOPMENTAL		
A. Planning or Design	1. To find out what problems face the target population; or how the problem is manifested or distributed in the target area or in similar situations; and/or how the target population views the problem; to see what is being done about the problem; to see what is involved. May include literature review to assess state of the art. To work out the details of how to carry out the program, select the method, who should be involved; to study pitfalls, chances of success, particular ways to deliver the method. To design the experimental situation for research.	1. Needs Assessment Survey Research Planning Grant Seed Money Grant Start-up Funds
B. Feasibility	2. To see if the target population would be receptive, if the method would be appropriate, if other anticipated conditions would come about. To see if research design is practicable.	2. Feasibility Study
C. Implementation	3. (a) Initial or new minimal installation of the method or model on a small scale; the purpose is not to test the method, but to get practical insight and to find "bugs." (b) First or new full-scale application of the method to a population, area or institution to show that the program works in this setting.	3. (a) Pilot Test (b) Demonstration Grant
II. OPERATIONAL	1. Beyond planning, design or implementation, when method has already been tested or is assumed to be effective. Part of the regular operations of the institution; day-to-day activities of the institution. Note: Funding is rarely given for general operations. When the government gives block, capitation or categoric grants for specific activities, competitive proposal writing is not required.	1. General Operating Funds Operating Grant Block Grant Capitation Grant Categoric Grant Entitlements
III. EVALUATION		
A. Formative	1. Done before a program is completed or method is tested, to find whether the program is being delivered as agreed; to test effectiveness of manner of delivery, efficiency, benefit/cost, reliability. Funds are not usually sought for formative evaluation because it is undertaken to	(a) Efficiency assessment: (cost per time period) (b) Benefit/cost analysis

continued

3

TABLE 1.1, continued

STAGE	PURPOSE	TYPE OF PROJECT
	improve program method or delivery. It is included in the evaluation design of grant proposals, and is done by an institution to improve functioning.	(c) Cost effectiveness (input/output) (d) Process evaluation (e) Program monitoring
B. Summative	2. To test whether the program has attained its stated program objectives; to decide whether to continue a program. In the latter case, the assessment may itself be the project proposed for funding, and the evaluating agency may be the same or different from the operating agency. May or may not include experimental or quasi-experimental design.	1. Program Evaluation
	3. The test of a clinical method to prove treatment success for a given class of clients. Usually experimental design.	2. Clinical Trial
	4. The test of a program method to prove a program's effectiveness for a stated population group or set of conditions. Usually quasi-experimental design. May compare test group with itself over time.	3. Program Trial

Notes: Training grants, staffing grants, capital grants, and grants for equipment are forms of proposals corresponding to start-up or expansion stages. They are relatively simple cases within other categories.

Experimental design and quasi-experimental design are used so that the results may be generalized to create new knowledge, used for hypothesis testing. Comparisons are made with alternative approaches and/or doing nothing. Experimental design involves use of random assignment to control groups, pre- and post-testing.

not available. Later, evaluation is done separately or as a preplanned phase, to test the efficacy of the methods employed and to assess whether the program's results and manner of delivery were as expected.

GETTING STARTED

The first thing to do is to decide on a project idea that you will try to get funded. You may already have a program you wish to fund, but if you do not have a project in mind, choose a program that the institution for which you work would like to see funded, but be selective. You may find it helpful to evaluate a project idea in terms of the following:

1. Is the subject one you know a good deal about, or will you have to spend time becoming familiar with the professional literature?

2. Is the idea something your organization or agency is interested in getting funded, so staff members will cooperate with you in your attempt to develop a realistic plan?

3. Is the idea significant? Does it help solve a serious problem for a population or institution? Is it of national importance? Will it fill a serious knowledge gap or be a major contribution to the field?

4. Can you talk about it? Even if you already have an idea for a grant proposal, you will have to meet with the people in your institution whose approval you need to go ahead. If you will be writing funding proposals for projects others will be directing, you will certainly have to meet with your agency people to make sure there is clarity on what the project will be, whom and how many it will serve, how long it will run, what its scope and methodology will be, and how much it will cost.

5. Determine why you and the agency are interested in this particular idea. What is the need for it? Why now? What stage of program development does it represent? This information is needed before you even begin to look for a potential funder because you need to know the context within which to search for funding sources.

   You know, for example, that you work for a hospital, senior citizens' center, religious institution, community development agency, or cultural, educational, or research institution. But being able to pinpoint the exact nature of the project idea, its stage of development, and its target population will enable you to find your way through the subject indexes around which most funding directories are organized and will help you with a starting idea of the amount of funding you will be seeking. You can then consider the particular project ideas of interest to the funding agencies and see if your initial idea can be adapted to fit what the funders are seeking to support.

6. You may wish to consider with your agency people the advantages and drawbacks of going for funding.

Drawbacks

If the chances are slim for funding, it may not be worth the time and effort required of the staff to develop the proposal.

Also, outside funding can create an unstable environment for the staff if their employment depends on "soft money." There can be a distortion of staffing patterns when an institution relies on such transient sources. Funding can distort the hierarchy of influence in favor of stars who bring in funds. Staff on year-to-year funding often leave for more secure jobs. The agency may not be able to continue operations once the funding ends.

Once funded, the agency may undergo change because it must conform to the funder's requirements, such as in its accounting system, reporting, outside monitors, type of service, clientele, and delivery methods. Your agency may lose its freedom to change direction or shift its time frame. The institution's policy can become subject to rapid shifts in funding priorities and fads in programs and may lose its integrity and the sense of its original mission.

Your agency may be asked to match funds beyond its means as a condition of being funded.

Your agency may not be prepared to disrupt its regular operations and staff assignments in order to mount the new program. Be sure all the departments involved are clear on the changes that would have to take place to run the new program.

Advantages

In working out the proposal, the agency can clarify its program goals, become more knowledgeable about the field, rethink "tried and tested" ways of providing service, and may even improve the program.

In having to conform to financial and reporting requirements, the agency may have an incentive to improve its administrative procedures.

In actually working through the stages of grant development, the agency may improve its support base and enhance its credibility and visibility with potential funding agencies. The staff learns to play the game, and contacts are made.

Even if you fail, you learn by doing. And, you might get funded!

7. To estimate the costs, count the time needed to research and develop the proposal, clerical and computer time, duplicating,

phone, visits to the funding agency, and consulting time. The costs of preparing a proposal are not reimbursable.

8. The time likely to be needed depends on the complexity of the application forms, the extent to which the writers know the literature and program details, the amount of support you must demonstrate, and the approval channels in your agency. This could take a week to several months. From the time a proposal is submitted to the point it is reviewed and a response is given can take several months. If you must go through preapplication and final application, more months are needed. Then you must wait before you can start until funds are actually made available. It all could take over a year.

9. What will be expected of you? And how do you feel about grant writing? In grant writing you assume the task of expressing the ideas and enthusiasm of the project's creator and the goals of your institution to an unknown audience at the funding agency. Your clarity of thought is critical. From the start you must be clear about your role in the grant-getting process from your agency's point of view.

In addition, if you have secret agendas involving people, ideas about how things will work out, or expect to have difficulty accepting criticism of your drafts, now is the time to bring these to the surface. You may not be able to change your feelings, but you can deal with them by making them conscious. These questions are posed now, when you have some idea about the project but while you still have time to make changes in the project or in the people you will involve. These questions are for you to deal with privately:

a. Will you be expected to do the planning and writing, coming to other staff members only for approvals and editorial responses, or are you expected to reflect the thinking of one or more principals? If the latter, how much will *your* ideas be respected? Will your inputs be seriously considered?

b. Will you be involved in planning meetings? In site visits? In visits to the funding agency?

c. Will you be coordinating the communication between your agency and the potential funding agencies, or will you be acting independently?

d. What support will you be given? Typing, duplicating, editorial feedback? Will you receive release time from your other duties?

e. Whose approval and involvement do you need? These may include the director or the one whose ideas are to be funded; key personnel who will staff the project and their supervisors; fiscal people; the key administrators who will "sign off" on the project; and those in the chain of formal approvals, including your supervisor and board members, if appropriate.

f. Are all these conditions acceptable to you?

g. Will you have cooperation from all the major staff in the agency who will be involved? Whom *must* you include? Whom *should* you include? How committed are they? Whom would you like to leave out? Why? What problems do you have to solve in relation to such people?

h. Will you be able to get inputs from target population representatives? Are you trying to avoid having yet another constituency to deal with?

i. How do you feel about asking for funding?
    "I should not have to do all this work. Just give it to me."
    "I am not good enough to get it."
    "Someone else should be doing all this."

j. Do you have a private agenda?
    A role you want to play in relation to people with whom you will deal.
    A new job in the proposed project.
    Support of hidden beliefs about the value of the program, or how one "gets it" (abundance).

k. Can you rid your mind of chaos and focus on:
    What you want to *give* to the program.
    The interests of the funding agency.
    The interests of the people who will be served by the program.

l. Does the project excite you?

10. *A Note on Revisions and Editorial Feedback.* Teachers and professors often accept confused, inarticulate, ungrammatical, and vague writing from students if they can grasp some glimmer of the student's meaning. Students get A's and B's for such work. But in the world of grant writing the readers are uninvolved, impersonal funding-agency staff members and reviewers, who will judge the applications in a competitive context. They will go only by what they understand the applicant to have written. Sometimes an agency requesting funds is so prestigious, and the need for a program so great, that bad writing is

overlooked, but as a rule the writer of grant proposals must submit well written, clear, and focused narratives that speak to the requirements of the funder.

What you need in order to get ready for such a situation is hard, constructive editorial feedback on English usage and logical flow in your writing. Find a person to provide this for you. It should be someone with good training whose own writing you can trust.

This means you must accept critical editing. For some people, especially those for whom being "perfect" has an emotional charge and for whom criticism is an attack on self, this is difficult. But please understand that the best writers have to revise; it is almost impossible to write grant proposals well in one sitting. That is why this book takes you through the process with several cumulative writing steps, to let you build toward the preapplication and the final proposal. You will benefit if you can free your defenses, not become rigid about redoing, and assume that feedback will be helpful.

One thing that helps release you to accept critical review is to work with a computer or word processor, since the idea of revision is then not so formidable. But in any case, assuming that each writing step will need revision will make it easier for you. Then go ahead and make the best use you can of your reviewer.

2

Funding Agencies

STARTING THE SEARCH

Once you have an approximate idea of your project and know who your target population is, you will want to find several appropriate funding agencies. You will want early input on your program's fundability and what is available.

Usually, institutional grant writers first decide on the program they want to get funded and then seek a funding agency that fits their interests. However, some agencies and grant writers start with the funding sources and design programs that fit the announced funding availabilities. The latter approach is dangerous for institutions because they run the risk of allowing the missions of their organizations to be subverted by following the fashions in grant giving — which follow political currents as well as public concerns.

You can develop a strategy that combines the two approaches. It is a good idea to look at potential funding sources as soon as you have an idea partly formulated; then you can see what the funding agencies are looking for and note the "buzz words" and the current hot issues in favor at the time. You can then fine-tune what you ask for to your best advantage, short of compromising the integrity of the project plan.

As an example, you may be dealing with drug dependency; drug-related AIDS transmission would be very much on the agenda for drug programs. Dealing with shared needles and sexual behavior would make your program more attractive and add to the significance of your work. However, suppose you were committed to caring for nondocumented laborers; if so, you might not want to accept funding that made disclosure a prerequisite for health care funds.

The sections that follow assume that you are starting out by looking for funds without an idea of which agency is likely to have funds for you. Three major sources are described, the federal government (and state pass-throughs), foundations, and corporations. (The latter two are known as the private sector.) Exhibit 1 presents five project ideas that will be followed as examples throughout the book.

EXHIBIT 1
Five Examples of Project Ideas

Example 1: Education for Parents of Infants Discharged from Intensive Care

You work for a hospital that has a neonatal intensive care unit. Before the infants are discharged, you wish to train the parents to deal with subsequent medical emergencies and to monitor for developmental problems. You also wish to provide basic parenting skills and referral to follow-up care after discharge. Your catchment area is a poor, inner-city community. You are looking for a project grant that will allow you to prepare the educational materials, let you train the mothers/caregivers of the infants in-house, and provide for follow-up care once the infants are discharged.

Example 2: Ambulance Staff Training in Emergency Medical Services

Your hospital wishes to train paramedical emergency medical care technicians in the use of a drug that has proven to be life saving for heart attack victims if given early enough. You want to ensure that your ambulance technologists can administer the drug safely and thereby save lives.

Example 3: City Children Involved in the Arts Community

You are a neighborhood association of artists living in an area known for its galleries and resident performing arts groups. You would like to promote community involvement in the arts by having artists and performers involved with children in the city's school system through performances, rehearsals, and work sessions in the artists' homes and performance spaces.

Example 4: Writing Skills for Retention of Graduate Students

You wish to fund writing courses and tutorial workshops for graduate students in health and human services programs. Professional programs at your college turn away candidates for admission or lose matriculants because the writing skills sufficient for their baccalaureate degrees are inadequate for masters-level work and the jobs for which the students wish to prepare. The aim is improved access and retention in a college that serves nontraditional working students, many with English as a second language and/or disadvantaged educational experiences.

continued

EXHIBIT 1, continued

Example 5: Development of Leadership by Women of Color in the Antiviolence Movement

Women of color form a large proportion of the recipients of programs dealing with domestic violence and sexual assault, but are not an organized force in the leadership of the agencies involved. Your nonprofit organization of volunteer women proposes to create task forces of women of color and provide the technical support needed to create culturally relevant models of intervention and ways to promote leadership among women of color in the antiviolence movement.

It is a good idea to look for potential funding in all sectors at first, even if you may have a lead. Such practice will give you the information you need to use the major reference sources for each category.

FEDERAL FUNDS

Over the years, federal funds have become increasingly specific in purpose. Of the five types of federal granting routes presented in Table 2.1, the first, unsolicited proposals, provides the offerer the most latitude. However, funding for unsolicited proposals is almost a thing of the past. The government's discretionary funds are increasingly offered through "requests for applications" (RFAs), which specify the purpose, scope of work, and criteria for funding, and "requests for proposals" (RFPs), which are even more prescriptive and result in contracts rather than grants. The result is that the government increasingly predetermines the direction and form of funded programs.

Even more specific is earmarked funding. For example, the competitive research grant program established by Congress in 1977 at the Department of Agriculture has generally been awarded through competitive peer review, designed to award grants by merit. However, for fiscal 1989, much of the funding was earmarked by Congress for specific agencies. A similar phenomenon occurs at the state level.

The funding period has also undergone restrictions. In the past, federal funding has often been available on a multiyear basis. When an applicant was awarded a grant, the first year's budget would be released, and the applicant agency would be given higher priority than new applicants in the subsequent years. Now, funding often goes to visible, one-year projects. This allows for more recipients and more political impact, but it limits projects that need development over a period of

TABLE 2.1

Federal Funding by Application Type

Form of Request/Support	Description	Comments

1. Unsolicited Proposal
   Your idea; you decide
   to contact agency.
   You get:
   GRANT
	Objectives of proposal match the funding agency's statements about subjects for which it will make funds available. No tight time deadline. Agency objectives can be found in agency literature.	Exploratory; the outcomes of project are unpredictable.

2. Response to a detailed Request for Application (RFA), or general announcement of fund availability. Usually has preapplication (preliminary proposal) phase and second-round final proposal phase.
   You get:
   GRANT
	Proposal must follow the prescribed order of presentation in timing and subject matter, but there is scope to apply innovative ideas within the framework. Stated criteria are used by reviewers, and meeting these is crucial. Deadline dates for applications, reviews and funding periods must be met. RFA in Federal Register, agency literature.	Specifically linked to stated list of desired outcomes.

3. Response to a detailed Request for Proposal (RFP) usually sent to preferred respected list of people and agencies, but also available to other bidders.
   You get:
   CONTRACT
	Not only the objectives, but tasks, methods and other aspects of the work are clearly specified. The object is for the funder to get what it wants carried out. Deadline dates for response. RFP's mailed or in Commerce Business Daily. Note: offerers may be invited to bidders conference, may be asked to write letters of intent.	RFP spells out the purpose, method, and products in detail.

4. RFP comes after an initial Request for Statement of Capability (RFSC) or	Funding agency solicits information on who is out there capable of doing the work to be solicited. There is a response deadline.	Competition to show ability to do the work, and get RFP.

RFP is tailored to an agency that the funder already has in mind. There is pre-RFP competition in both cases.
   You get:
   CONTRACT
	Funding agency is convinced that a particular institution has a unique plan or capability; but in order to fulfill requirement for competitive bidding RFP is designed to fit the chosen offerer's particular features. Time period is that of the RFP, but offerer has probably already done much of the preparation.	RFP tailored to offerer's design because it fits funder's needs.

5. Sole Source Provider
   You get:
   CONTRACT
	No competition because no one else can deliver what the funder needs. Initiated by either funder or offerer.	Contract for what offerer is equipped to do.

years. The New York Public Library was turned down for three-year funding in June 1988, after 16 years of matching-funds support, on the grounds that grants must be limited to specific one-year projects.

However, federal funds are still the most coveted, because federal agencies remain relatively open and competitive in their award processes, and the awards can be large. Federal agencies are required to provide funding applications to all who request them, and to provide reasons, on request, for acceptance or rejection. The price paid for this is that the applications require the most complex and lengthy formal proposals of all sources of funding.

Applicants Eligible to Receive Federal Funds

The federal government makes awards to six classes of recipients through fifteen forms of support, not all of which are monetary. In June 1988 there were approximately 1,043 support programs being run by the federal government. Each had about three types of recipients. The distribution of the programs by recipient agency is presented in Table 2.2.

TABLE 2.2
Distribution of Federal Assistance Programs by
Eligibility, June 1988

Types of Recipients Eligible for Assistance	Programs	Percent
1. State: Any agency or instrumentality of the fifty States, and the District of Columbia. State does not include the political subdivisions of the State, but does include institutions of higher education and hospitals.	691	66%
2. Nonprofit: A public or private agency or organization established by charter to perform specialized functions or services for the benefit of all or part of the general public. Functions or services are provided without charge or at cost, and earn no profit. The agency or organization has no shareholders to receive dividends.	596	57
3. Individual: Any person or persons, as individuals, groups, or profit making organizations. Such persons or groups do not represent federally recognized Indian tribal governments. Includes Indians or other Native Americans who apply as individuals rather than as members of a tribe or other Indian organization.	523	50

continued

TABLE 2.2, continued

Types of Recipients Eligible for Assistance	Programs	Percent
4. Local: Agencies or instrumentalities of political subdivisions within a State, to include cities, towns, townships, parishes, municipalities, villages, counties, school districts, and other special local districts. Included are Indian tribes on State reservations, Indian bands and groups, Pueblos, Indian school boards, and State-designated Indian tribes. Excluded are institutions of higher education and hospitals.	496	48
5. U.S. Territories: Any agency or instrumentality of the Commonwealth of Puerto Rico, the Virgin Islands, Guam, American Samoa, the Trust Territories of the Pacific Islands, and the Mariana Islands. Included are the political subdivisions of the territories, institutions of higher learning, and hospitals.	312	30
6. Federally Recognized Indian Tribal Organizations: The governing body or a governmental agency of an Indian tribe, nation, or other organized group or community recognized and certified by the Secretary of the Interior. Included are native villages as defined in the Alaska Native Claims Settlement Act.	213	20
Total Programs*	1,043	

Source: Executive Office of the President, Office of Management and Budget, *1988 Catalog of Federal Domestic Assistance* (Washington, D.C.: General Services Administration, June 1988), pp. AEI-1–AEI-22.

*Numbers do not add to the total because programs have multiple recipients.

As Table 2.2 shows, and as concurrent federal assistance policies have made clear, the states are major recipients of federal support, with the power to distribute within the states. The states claimed assistance under 66 percent of the programs. Local governments were entitled to apply for help in 48 percent of the programs, giving government a role in most programs. Nonprofit organizations, which include health care providers; research institutions; neighborhood centers; museums; cultural societies; theater troupes; schools; welfare agencies; centers for children, the elderly, or the handicapped; environmentally oriented groups; and legal aid associations, among others, could apply for help in 57 percent of the programs. What may come as a surprise to many is that 50 percent of the programs also allowed support to individuals and profit-making organizations.

Types of Support

The federal government provides fifteen types of support, of which only seven include financial assistance. The other eight are as follows.

Sale, Exchange, or Donation of Property and Goods

Use of Property, Facilities, and Equipment

Provision of Specialized Services

Advisory Services and Counseling

Dissemination of Technical Information

Training

Investigation of Complaints

Federal Employment

Forms of support such as Dissemination of Technical Information, which can include educational material and reports, and Use of Property, Facilities, and Equipment, which might not be available under project grants, can be useful when put together with other forms of support.

Of the seven forms of financial support, five are very restricted in form.

Direct Payments for Specific Use — to encourage a particular activity.

Direct Payments with Unrestricted Use — such as retirement, pension, and compensation

Direct Loans

Guaranteed/Insured Loans

Insurance

Formula Grants — Formula grants, the sixth type of financial support, include allocations of money to government entities according to prescribed formulae for activities of a continuous nature. They are not confined to a specific project and are sometimes called entitlements. (See Table 1.1, under "Operational.") However, some of these may require competitive applications within the state, when the funds are earmarked as discretionary funds under the term *block grants*.

Project Grants — Project grants are the form of federal financial support that grant writers usually seek, the seventh type. In 1988 only 526, 50 percent of federal assistance programs, contained a project-grant component. Project grants vary in size and in the extent to which they are earmarked for particular activities, such as research or social services, or particular recipients.

Sources of Information

The major source book for federal funding is the current *Catalog of* *Federal Domestic Assistance*. (See Selected Bibliography.) It is available at federal depository libraries and most research libraries, as well as at the Foundation Center, the local office of which is the single best place to go for research on foundation and corporate funding. (See the section on foundations later in this chapter.) The annual *Catalog of Federal Domestic Assistance* has a midyear supplement, usually placed in front of the original text in libraries.

Within the *Catalog,* programs are keyed with a multidigit decimal code number, and that is how they are listed within the indexes. The type of support given is shown in indexes by a letter in parentheses. If you already have a project idea, you use the Federal Agency, Functional, or Subject indexes to find possible programs. To find the program descriptions, you enter the main text, where the programs are presented in numerical order.

The program descriptions have categories such as, Name, Federal Agency, Enabling Legislation, Objectives, Types of Assistance, Uses and Restrictions, Eligibility Requirements, Application and Award Process, Special Requirements and Restrictions, Financial Requirements, History of Past Awards, Regulations and Guidelines, Regional and Headquarter Contacts, Related Programs, Examples of Funded Programs, and Criteria for Selecting Proposals. There is also information on special federal circular policies (usually related to fiscal reporting or intergovernmental review) and deadlines. Sometimes the criteria include evaluation design specifications.

A note of caution: Do not consider the deadline dates definitive, since they are frequently revised after publication of the *Catalog.*

The *Catalog Supplement* contains a table of contents, revisions, and updating instructions, a summary list of modified programs, a list of deleted and added programs, new program descriptions, and new indexes. The updated indexes and new program descriptions are usually added to the front of the volume, and the old program descriptions remain. So if you are browsing, check the new indexes, which tell which programs have been deleted and which added, to be sure about a given program.

The *Federal Register* publishes the federal government's RFAs and regulations regarding funding, as well as changes in deadlines. The *Commerce Business Daily* is the source for published RFPs. If you know which federal agency funds the kind of program you are interested in, the publications of that agency provide the best information on funding. (See also the Selected Bibliography in this book.)

Examples Using the *Catalog of Federal Domestic Assistance*

You may recall that you were encouraged to have some idea of the project you will try to get funded. Five examples were presented in Exhibit 1. This section uses three to show how you can use the *Catalog*.

Example 1: Education for Parents of Infants Discharged from Intensive Care

When you skim the Agency Index, you find two likely agencies listed under "Department of Health and Human Services." They are the Public Health Service (PHS) and the Office of Human Development Services (OHDS). Under PHS you see that there are project grants, coded as such by the descriptive letter *B*. One, shown as relevant to "Maternal and Child Health," is number 13.110, listed as "Maternal and Child Health Federal Consolidated Programs." Little seems relevant under OHDS.

The Functional Index lists a category under "Health" called "Education and Training," but there is nothing under patient or client training. However, you find number 13.110 there, as well as under "Maternity, Infants, Children." The other titles seem to be focused on other issues. Under "Specialized Health Research and Training," you again find 13.110, and nothing else that seems relevant. Using the Subject Index, you find "Maternity, Infant Care," 10.557; "Medical Services," 13.110, 13.994; and "Preventive Services," 13.135, 13.136, 13.144, and 13.283.

Now you are ready to examine the program descriptions. Examining the programs in numerical order, here is what you find:

Program Number	Finding
10.557	Deals with food, not applicable.
13.110	Special Project Grants seems to apply.
13.135	Prevention Centers, not applicable.
13.136	Injury Control, not applicable.
13.144	Drug and Alcohol Abuse, not applicable.
13.283	Technical Assistance, not Project Grants.
13.994	Formula Grants, not applicable.

Is there a match between your project idea and a federal program? One program seems appropriate. Its *Catalog* description is presented in Exhibit 2.

EXHIBIT 2
Example of Federal Program Description in *Catalog of Federal Domestic Assistance,* 1988: Maternal and Child Health

NUMBER: 13.110
NAME: Maternal and Child Health Federal Consolidated Programs.
          (Special Projects of Regional and National Significance (SPRANS)).
FEDERAL AGENCY: Health Resources and Services Administration, Public Health
          Service, Department of Health and Human Services.
AUTHORIZATION: Social Security Act, as amended, Title V, Section 502(a)(1),42
          U.S.C. 702.
OBJECTIVES:
          To carry out special projects of regional and national significance,
          training, and research; conduct genetic disease testing, counseling, and
          information development and dissemination programs; and support comprehensive
          hemophilia diagnostic and treatment centers.
TYPES OF ASSISTANCE: Project Grants.
USES AND USE RESTRICTIONS: Training grants are made to institutions of higher
          learning for training personnel for health care and related services for
          mothers and children. Research grants are for purposes of research activities
          related to (CSHCN)(both elements of 13.994, Maternal and Child Health Services
          Block Grant) which show promise of a substantial contribution to the
          advancement of service programs. Genetic grants are for genetic disease
          testing, counseling and information development and dissemination. Hemophilia
          grants are for the support of centers which provide hemophilia diagnostic and
          treatment services. Special Project Grants are designed to support activities
          of a demonstration nature which pertain to Maternal and Child Health and CSHCN
          programs. *

*13.994, under Beneficiary Eligibility, lists: "Mothers, infants and children, particularly of low income families." Under Uses and Use Restrictions it is stated that "funds may not be used for (1) inpatient services other than those provided to children with special health care needs or to high risk pregnant women and infants and such other inpatient services as the Secretary may approve."

continued

ELIGIBILITY REQUIREMENTS:

Applicant Eligibility: Training grants may be made to public or nonprofit private institutions of higher learning. Research grants may be made to public or nonprofit institutions of higher learning and public or nonprofit private agencies and organizations engaged in research or in Maternal and Child Health or CSHCN programs. Any public or private entity is eligible for hemophilia and genetics grants Special Projects Grants of Regional and National Significance.

Beneficiary Eligibility: For Training grants: (1) trainees in the health professions; and (2) mothers and children who receive services through training programs. For research grants: same as applicant eligibility. For hemophilia, genetics and special projects: (1) public or private agencies, organizations and institutions; and (2) mothers and children who receive services through the programs.

Credentials/Documentation: Proof of nonprofit status is required. Costs will be determined in accordance with OMB Circular No. A-87 for State and local governments. For other grantees, costs will be determined by HHS Regulations 45 CFR 74, Subpart Q.

APPLICATION AND AWARD PROCESS:

Preapplication Coordination: Not applicable. This program is excluded from coverage under E.O. 12372.

Application Procedure: Informal inquiries regarding the program and intent to submit an application should be directed to the headquarters office. The standard application forms, as furnished by DHHS and required by OMB Circular No. A-102 for State and local governments, must be used for this program. Application procedures differ by subprogram category and may be obtained from the Headquarters Office (see listing below for address). This program is subject to the provisions of OMB Circulars No. A-102 and No. A-110, as appropriate.

Award Procedure: Project applications are reviewed by members of the staff of DHHS and by a non-governmental review committee of experts. Applications are reviewed for merit and are then recommended for approval or disapproval. Final decisions regarding approval are made by the Associate Bureau Director of the Office for Maternal and Child Health.

Deadlines: March 1 through August 1, depending upon the specific program. Consult Headquarters Office.

Range of Approval/Disapproval Time: 4 months.

Appeals: Applicant may reapply for support if revised applications are submitted.

Renewals: After initial award, projects may be renewed annually depending on submission and approval of a satisfactory application.

ASSISTANCE CONSIDERATIONS:

Formula and Matching Requirements: This program has no statutory formula or matching requirements.

Length and Time Phasing of Assistance: Awards are made on an annual basis. The award will normally be in one lump sum for the entire grant period and payments are made through an Electronic Transfer System or Cash Demand System.

POST ASSISTANCE REQUIREMENTS:

Reports: Annual program reports, annual financial status reports, annual program service reports and special reports as required.

Audits: In accordance with the provisions of OMB Circular No. A-128, "Audits of State and Local Governments," State and local governments that receive financial assistance of $100,000 or more within the State's fiscal year shall have an audit made for that year. State and local governments that receive between $25,000 and $100,000 within the State's fiscal year shall have an audit made in accordance with Circular No. A-128, or in accordance with Federal laws and regulations governing the programs in which they participate. For nongovernmental grant recipients, audits are to be carried out in accordance with the provisions set forth in OMB Circular No. A-110. In addition, grants and cooperative agreements are subject to inspection and audits by DHHS and other Federal officials.

continued

EXHIBIT 2, continued

Records: HHS and the Comptroller General of the United States or any of their
authorized representatives, shall have the right of access to any books,
documents, papers or other records of a grantee, sub-grantee, contractor
or subcontractor, which are pertinent to the HHS grant, in order to make
audits, examinations, excerpts and transcripts. In accordance with 45 CFR
Part 74, Subpart D, grantees are required to maintain grant accounting
records 3 years after the end of a budget period. If any litigation,
claim, negotiation, audit or other action involving the record has been
started before the expiration of the 3-year period, the records shall be
retained until completion of the action and resolution of all issues which
arise from it, or until the end of the regular 3-year period, whichever is
later.

FINANCIAL INFORMATION:
    Account Identification: 75-0350-0-1-551.
    Obligations: (Grants) FY 87 $75,625; FY 88 est $82,288,260; and FY 89 est
    $90,499,000.
    Range and Average of Financial Assistance: $50,000 to $1,000,000; $174,000.
PROGRAM ACCOMPLISHMENTS: In fiscal year 1987, 703 applications were received and a
    total of 460 projects were funded. In fiscal year 1988, it is anticipated
    that 490 projects will be funded. It is anticipated that 536 projects will be
    funded in fiscal year 1989. A wide variety of services were provided to
    thousands of mothers and children, including counseling, diagnostic,
    therapeutic, and other secondary and tertiary level services.
REGULATIONS, GUIDELINES, AND LITERATURE: Pertinent information may be obtained by
    contacting the Headquarters Office indicated below.
INFORMATION CONTACTS:
    Regional or Local Office: Not applicable.
    Headquarters Office: Division for Maternal and Child health, Health Resources
    and Services Administration, Public Health Service, Room 6-05, 5600
    Fishers Lane, Rockville, MD 20857. Telephone: (301) 443-2170.
    (Actually, 443-1440 for applications (ed.).) (Use same 7-digit number for
    FTS.) Contact: Vince L. Hutchins, MD.
RELATED PROGRAMS: 13.994, Maternal and Child Health Services Block Grant.
EXAMPLES OF FUNDED PROJECTS: 1) Health Professional Training Projects; 2) Schools
    of Public Health; 3) Maternal and Child Health Research; 4) Genetic Screening,
    Testing and Counseling; 5) Hemophilia diagnosis and treatment centers; and 6)
    Child and Adolescent Health Services Demonstration Projects.
CRITERIA FOR SELECTING PROPOSALS: Criteria are included in the program guidance
    materials provided with the application kits. Contact Headquarters Office for
    details.

Source: Catalog of Federal Domestic Assistance, 1988.

Here is what you can learn from the program description presented in
Exhibit 2. From reading the Objectives you learn that because infant
mortality is a national issue, and your target population is disadvantaged,
high-risk infants, you may qualify as a special project of national
significance. If you provide a good evaluation design that can show the
effectiveness of the program, you may have a research component.

The funding *is* in the form of project grants. Look at Uses and Use
Restrictions. If you were a research grantee you would be dealing with
the advancement of service programs. Your population group is,
appropriately, low-income families, and you would be providing services
to children with special health care needs and high-risk infants. (See

footnote, Exhibit 2.) If you were a special project grantee, you would be able to mount the project as a demonstration grant, which would put fewer experimental research demands on you. That would be best, since the methodology is not ready for program trial. Your interests are definitely within the Maternal and Child Health purview. A special project grant it is!

What about *Eligibility*? The hospital is a nonprofit public foundation, and the beneficiaries are the agency and the mothers and children who receive Children with Special Health Needs (CSHN) services. You are OK.

The Examples of Funded Projects section is an additional check that you are in the right place. This program tells less than most descriptions, but Number 6 indicates that a child health service demonstration project will be acceptable. Clearly, you *must* call and get the application, regulations, and guidelines from the contact person at the headquarters office in Washington, D.C.

The Comments under Program Accomplishments reinforce the likelihood that what you wish to do will be attractive to the agency, but only seeing the application and the actual criteria for selecting proposals will tell you what they want.

What else can you learn? You will not be subjected to intergovernmental review (described in Chapter 3). You will be able to get informal feedback and will even be able to submit an informal discussion paper should you so desire (Application Procedure). There is no preapplication phase. You probably need a three-year grant, but you will only be able to count on funds for one year at a time. The approximate sum you can ask for a given year can be very high, but around $174,000 is a safe figure.

Example 3: City Children Involved in the Arts Community

The Agency Index in the *Catalog* lists the National Endowment for the Arts, under which you find a program for "Inter-Arts." The Functional Index, under "Cultural Affairs, Promotion of the Arts," has programs, as does the Subject Index, under "Arts, General, Special Projects." One program that appears in each seems to be appropriate. It is presented in Exhibit 3.

Is there a match between your project idea and a federal program? From the Objectives you see that your project must have potential national or regional impact. This is likely if you are able to develop a model for use in similar communities over the nation. Uses and Restrictions tells

EXHIBIT 3
Example of Federal Program Description in *Catalog of Federal Domestic Assistance*, 1988: Inter-Arts

NUMBER: 45.011

NAME: Promotion of the Arts -- Inter-Arts.

FEDERAL AGENCY: National Endowment for the Arts, National Foundation on the Arts and the Humanities.

AUTHORIZATION: National Foundation on the Arts and the Humanities Act of 1965, as amended, Public Law 89-209, 20 U.S.C. 951 et seq..

OBJECTIVES: To provide grants for projects that involve two or more art forms and that have potential national or regional impact.

TYPES OF ASSISTANCE: Project Grants.

USES AND USE RESTRICTIONS: Grants may be used for projects which involve two, or more art forms, which meet professional standards and have potential national or regional significance. Included is assistance for presenting organizations, artists' colonies, interdisciplinary arts projects, arts service organizations, and State arts agencies and regional arts organizations. Support is also provided for dance presentations through cooperative programs with 45.002, Promotion of the Arts -- Dance and 45.007, Promotion of the Arts --State Programs.

ELIGIBILITY REQUIREMENTS:

Applicant Eligibility: Grants may be made only to nonprofit organizations if donations to such organizations qualify as a charitable deduction under Section 170(c) of the Internal Revenue Code. This definition also includes States, local governments, State arts agencies and regional arts organizations. There are no grants to individuals.

Beneficiary Eligibility: Nonprofit organizations including State and local governments, State arts agencies, and regional arts organizations.

Credentials/Documentation: Copy of Internal Revenue Service tax exemption determination letter (in case of nonprofit organization). Costs will be determined in accordance with OMB Circular No. A-87 for State and local governments. For institutions of higher education, allowable costs will be determined according to OMB Circular No. A-21; for other nonprofit organizations making application, allowable costs will be determined according to OMB Circular No. A-122.

APPLICATION AND AWARD PROCESS:

Preapplication Coordination: This program is excluded from coverage under OMB Circular No. A-102. This program is excluded from coverage under E.O. 12372.

Application Procedure: Applicants should request information for this program area and standard application forms (NEA-3 for organizations) from headquarters office. This program is subject to the provisions of OMB Circular No. A-110.

Award Procedure: The Chairman of the Endowment makes final decision on all awards based on recommendations from National Council on the Arts (the NEA advisory body) and consulting panels in this field. Headquarters office will determine on a case-by-case basis those initial applicants that can further disburse grant money.

Deadlines: Presenting Organizations and Dance/Inter-Arts/State program - May 20, 1988; Partnerships in Touring and Commissioning - May 9, 1988; Interdisciplinary Arts Projects - February 6, 1989; Services to the Arts and Artists Colonies - November 4, 1988.

Range of Approval/Disapproval Time: Dependent on meetings of National Council on the Arts.

Appeals: Information on the appeals process may be obtained from the headquarters office listed below.

Renewals: Renewal grants may be made and are processed as new applications.

ASSISTANCE CONSIDERATIONS:

Formula and Matching Requirements: Grants to organizations, with few exceptions, must be matched at least dollar-for-dollar with nonfederal funds.

continued

Length and Time Phasing of Assistance: Length and time may vary with project. Generally, requests may be received at any time for payment to cover immediate expenses.

POST ASSISTANCE REQUIREMENTS:

Reports: A financial report within 90 days after termination of grant or as requested, plus narrative of accomplishment must be submitted.

Audits: Provided in accordance with the provisions of OMB Circular No. A-110 for organizations other than State and local governments. In accordance with the provisions of OMB Circular No. A-128, "Audits of State and Local Governments," State and local governments that receive financial assistance of $100,000 or more within the State's fiscal year shall have an audit made for that year. State and local governments that receive between $25,000 and $100,000 within the State's fiscal year shall have an audit made in accordance with Circular No. A-128, or in accordance with Federal laws and regulations governing the programs in which they participate.

Records: Financial records to be retained by grantee for three years following submission of final reports.

FINANCIAL INFORMATION:

Account Identification: 59-0100-0-1-503.

Obligations: (Grants) FY 87 $4,044.305; FY 88 est $4,100,000; and FY 89 est $4,300,000.

Range and Average of Financial Assistance: Organizations: Most grants range from $5,000 to $50,000 in fiscal years 1987, 1988 and 1989. Average grants range from $10,000 and $20,000.

PROGRAM ACCOMPLISHMENTS: In fiscal year 1987, 542 applications were received; 224 grants were awarded. In fiscal year 1988, we anticipate receiving 534 applications and awarding 227 grants. In fiscal year 1989, we anticipate receiving 540 applications and awarding 230 grants.

REGULATIONS, GUIDELINES, AND LITERATURE: The following are available from Public Information, National Endowment for the Arts, 1100 Pennsylvania Avenue, NW., Washington, DC 20506: "National Endowment for the Arts," and "Inter-Arts Guidelines."

INFORMATION CONTACTS:

Regional or Local Office: None.

Headquarters Office: Director, Inter-Arts Program, National Endowment for the Arts, 1100 Pennsylvania Avenue, NW., Washington, DC 20506. Telephone: (202) 682-5444 (use same 7-digit number for FTS).

RELATED PROGRAMS: 45.001, Promotion of the Arts -- Design Arts; 45.002 Promotion of the Arts -- Dance; 45.003, Promotion of the Arts -- Arts in Education; 45.004 Promotion of the Arts -- Literature; 45.005, Promotion of the Arts -- Music; 45.006 Promotion of the Arts -- Media Arts: Film/Radio/Television; 45.007, Promotion of the Arts -- State Programs; 45.008, Promotion of the Arts -- Theater; 45.009 Promotion of the Arts -- Visual Arts; 45.010, Promotion of the Arts -- Expansion Arts; 45.014 Promotion of the Arts -- Opera-Musical Theater; 45.015, Promotion of the Arts -- Folk Arts.

EXAMPLES OF FUNDED PROJECTS: To support arts presentations by Performing Art Centers and assist them in building audiences and patrons; (2) for residency fellowships at artists' colonies for a wide range of artists including writers, composers and visual artists; (3) to support presenter service organizations for strengthening the presenter within the community it serves; (4) to support organizations which sponsor collaborative, interdisciplinary arts projects; (5) to support service activities designed to develop financial and volunteer support for the arts, to expand skills and resources of developing arts institutions, and to disseminate information to artists and art administrators.

CRITERIA FOR SELECTING PROPOSALS: All applications are reviewed according to the following standards: artistic quality, the merit of the project, the applicants capacity to accomplish it, and evidence of local support for the project.

Source: Catalog of Federal Domestic Assistance, 1988.

you that professional art standards must be met. Since you are dealing with established, recognized artists and companies, you are OK. And you *do* qualify as an arts service organization, able to receive charitable donations under the law.

Looking at Examples of Funded Projects, you identify yourself as a project that will be building future audiences. The criteria, artistic quality, project merit, ability to accomplish, and evidence of local support, can be met if you show the interest and readiness to participate on the part of the schools involved, the school boards, and the department of education.

What else can you learn? There is no preapplication phase. Informal consultation will be available from the funding agency's staff. No intergovernmental review (E.O. 12372) is required. Renewal grant applications are treated as new ones.

The important information here is that grants to organizations require one-to-one matches from other sources, with few exceptions. This means pursuing informal contacts at the agency to discover whether you are eligible for an exception and/or for finding matching funds from foundations, local schools, private donations, or the public. This is a serious consideration, especially since the average grant is only $10,000 to $20,000.

Example 4: Writing Skills for Retention of Graduate Students

In the Agency Index of the *Catalog,* the Department of Education has one likely program. It is described in Exhibit 4.

EXHIBIT 4
Example of Federal Program Description in *Catalog of Federal Domestic Assistance,* **1988: Graduate Education**

NUMBER: 84.116
NAME: Fund for the Improvement of Postsecondary Education (FIPSE).
FEDERAL AGENCY: Office of Assistant Secretary for Postsecondary Education, Department of Education.
AUTHORIZATION: Higher Education Act of 1965, Title X, as amended, 20 U.S.C. 1135-1135a-3.
OBJECTIVES: To provide assistance for innovative programs which improve the access to and quality of postsecondary education.
TYPES OF ASSISTANCE: Project Grants.
USES AND USE RESTRICTIONS: The Fund provides project grants for activities sponsored by institutions and agencies which develop and demonstrate more effective approaches to the provision of postsecondary education. Priority is given to activities which relate to: (1) Improvement of undergraduate liberal arts education; (2) broad dissemination and impact. Consideration, but low

continued

priority, is given to requests for student aid and equipment. Construction costs will not be considered.

ELIGIBILITY REQUIREMENTS:

Applicant Eligibility: The full range of providers of postsecondary educational services including but not limited to: two and four-year colleges and universities, community organizations, libraries, museums, consortia, student groups, and local government agencies.

Beneficiary Eligibility: New and Existing postsecondary educational institutions and organizations; accredited and non-accredited.

Credentials/Documentation: This program is excluded from coverage under OMB Circular A-87.

APPLICATION AND AWARD PROCESS:

Preapplication Coordination: Recommend contact with the Fund directly. Application forms are furnished by the Fund. This program is excluded from coverage under OMB Circular No. A-102. This program is excluded from coverage under E.O. 12372.

Application Procedure: There is a two stage proposal process. Preliminary proposals are submitted directly to to the Fund. These five page documents state the problem to be addressed, provide a description of the program, indicate an evaluation format and list a budget. This program is subject to the provisions of OMB Circular No. A-110. Successful preliminary applicants are invited to submit final proposals.

Award Procedure: Proposals are reviewed by field readers, by staff, by the Board of the Fund, by the Director, and by appropriate Departmental officials. State Postsecondary Education Commissions must be given an opportunity to comment on projects funded in their States.

Deadlines: The deadlines have not been established.

Range of Approval/Disapproval Time: From one to four months.

Appeals: None.

Renewals: Applications for renewal of multi-year projects are processed and funded before those for new projects.

ASSISTANCE CONSIDERATIONS:

Formula and Matching Requirements: The Fund suggests that some institutional funds be included as part of program support, but this is not required by current legislation or regulation.

Length and Time Phasing of Assistance: The Fund will support multi-year projects on a declining fund basis; grants are awarded on a one to three year basis, with phasing of assistance as required. Funds are released as required.

POST ASSISTANCE REQUIREMENTS:

Reports: The Fund will require periodic progress evaluation reports from grant recipients, as well as a final report upon termination of funding.

Audits: Compliance with standard Education Department audit requirements.

Records: Grant recipients will be required to maintain standard financial records.

FINANCIAL INFORMATION:

Account Identification: 91-0201-0-1-502.

Obligations: (Grants) FY 87 $12,163,000; FY 88 est $11,645,000; and FY 89 est $13,645,000.

Range and Average of Financial Assistance: $5,000 to $150,000; $70,000 average.

PROGRAM ACCOMPLISHMENTS: In fiscal year 1987, out of 2,120 proposals, the Fund awarded 78 new grants and 98 continuation grants.

REGULATIONS, GUIDELINES, AND LITERATURE: Program information document published annually; regulations are found in the Federal Register. Program information and application procedures for the 1988 program are available as of October.

INFORMATION CONTACTS:

Regional or Local Office: Not applicable.

Headquarters Office: Fund for the Improvement of Postsecondary Education, Office of the Assistant Secretary for Postsecondary Education, 7th and D Streets, SW., ROB-3, Room 3100, Washington, DC 20202. Contact: Constance Cook. Telephone: (202) 245-8091.

continued

EXHIBIT 4, continued

RELATED PROGRAMS: None.

EXAMPLES OF FUNDED PROJECTS: 1) Improved undergraduate liberal arts curriculum; 2) improved undergraduate teaching; 3) liberalizing graduate education; 4) improved access for Blacks, Hispanics and other minorities; 5) cooperation between colleges and businesses; 6) teacher education; and 7) uses of technology.

CRITERIA FOR SELECTING PROPOSALS: 1) Its comparative contribution to the Fund's general criteria (learner-centeredness, broad impact, cost-effectiveness); 2) its comparative contribution to the relevant program objectives; 3) the extent to which, in meeting these goals, the project represents an improvement upon, or significant departure from, existing practice; 4) the extent to which the project involves processes, features, or products applicable in other postsecondary educational settings; 5) the feasibility of its project design, including budget and evaluation plans; 6) evidence of commitment to the proposed activity, including, when appropriate,, institutional cost-sharing; 7) its potential for continuation after Fund support (unless it is self-terminating); and 8) its appropriateness for Fund support in terms of the availability of other external funding sources for the proposed activities.

Source: Catalog of Federal Domestic Assistance, 1988.

Is there a match between your project idea and a federal program? The Objectives ask for innovative programs that improve access to and quality of postsecondary education. Remediation has traditionally been confined to the undergraduate curriculum, but graduate education is not ruled out. While priority is given to liberal arts undergraduate education, this also need not rule out your project. The Examples section includes liberalizing graduate education and improving access for minorities. You certainly fit there.

The Criteria section includes learner-centeredness; cost-effectiveness; evaluation design; applicability elsewhere; evidence of commitment, including cost-sharing; potential for continuation after funding; and appropriateness. The proposal would clearly have to address these areas, and so would the project design. The chance of being funded for the first time is roughly one out of ten for new proposals. An average grant is about $70,000.

What else can you learn? This program has a two-step procedure requiring a preapplication limited to five pages. Prior contact with the agency would seem to make sense. Grantee contributions are not required by law but are clearly called for. Multiyear funding is available but involves decreasing levels of support over time, up to three years. No intergovernmental review (E.O. 12372) is required.

Block Grants, Formula Grants, Contracts, and State Funding

Formula Grants

As indicated earlier, formula grants provide allocations of money to states and their subdivisions according to formulas prescribed by law or administrative regulation, for activities usually of an ongoing nature. The formulas may include population size, number of eligible beneficiaries, or prior allocations in a given program for a given year. The states must apply, but the applications are not competitive. The states generally determine a system for the distribution of the funds, which go directly to organizations that will undertake to provide the eligible services. In most of the *Catalog* indexes, formula grants are listed with the symbol (A) after the program name.

Block Grants

Block grants are sums available to states to accomplish specific aims of programs and are restricted with respect to the beneficiaries of the services they fund. States may receive the funds according to a formula and may use the funds directly or award them through grants or contracts to other public or private organizations. States establish their own application procedures. The grants can be located in the *Catalog* indexes by the words "Block Grant" as part of the program name. In 1988, of 17 block grants in the *Catalog,* 12 were formula grants (A); 6 were project grants (B); and three were direct-payment grants (C). (Some were of two types.) The Department of Health and Human Services had 10 block grants; the Department of Housing and Urban Development had 5; and the Department of Justice and the Department of Education each had one.

If you are eligible under a formula grant, you might be notified by the state or you might have to seek out the relevant state department; the latter is more likely to be your route under block grants, which makes it a more difficult process.

Contracts

Contracts, which are more specific in what they require from the recipient than project grants, are announced in the publications distributed by the federal agency. Another place to look for announcements of RFPs is the *Commerce Business Daily,* but you can also get on mailing lists for

RFPs from specific government agencies. For example, the National Institutes of Health publishes the *NIH Guide for Grants and Contracts* for individuals and organizations who wish to keep informed of opportunities and changing requirements for grant and contact funding. Other agencies have similar publications. There are also private bulletins that report on grants and contracts, such as the *Federal Grants & Contracts Weekly*, and specialized private bulletins for education, the arts, and health, among others.

State Funding

Aside from block-grant pass-throughs, state funds are available through organizations such as councils on children and families, councils on the arts, and the various departments of state government. There are few directories that include state governments among their lists of sources, but you should check the directories for your particular state to be sure.

FOUNDATIONS

Foundations are the second most important source of project support. They are private or public nonprofit agencies intended to contribute to public well-being by specific forms of service. *Operating foundations* use resources to contribute directly, by conducting research or providing services. Yours is probably an operating foundation. *Nonoperating foundations* are the ones we normally think of as foundations. They give money to recipient applicants to accomplish their goals and are the funding agencies. To receive funds, your organization must be a private operating foundation or a public foundation. All tax-exempt foundations are treated as private unless they apply for public status. You receive your status as a nonprofit organization and as a public or private foundation through application to the Internal Revenue Service.

With the tightening of federal funds in the 1980s, there has been increased pressure on foundations (and corporations) to take up the slack. However, together these two sources of funds represent no more than 10 percent of total philanthropic giving, and the gap has not been filled. The result, with few exceptions, is that foundations tend to be conservative in their grants policies, preferring to provide money to known successes. With so many "orphaned" programs, there is little room for new or unconventional ones. However, there have been some new foundations formed that specifically address issues such as promotion of peace, women's issues, and support for local community activism and initiative.

The incentive for foundation giving is the force of law, which requires private foundations to pay out the equivalent of 5 percent of their assets every year. In times of increasing asset valuation, the pot grows. Table 2.3, on foundations, presents the various types of foundations and their interests. Note that although operating funds are almost impossible to get, they are sometimes available from community foundations for support of ongoing operations of local worth.

There are from 22,000 to 29,000 foundations in the United States. Of these, about 5,150 have assets of $1 million or more or give over $100,000 in annual grants. Given the large differences in size, there are differences in policies and accessibility. The larger foundations, which usually have full-time or part-time staffs, can offer information and guidance by telephone, frequent board meetings, printed guidelines, and the counsel of professional staff members. The largest foundations provide competitive structures for the application process, and with less red tape than the federal government. The small foundations are hard to get information from and have infrequent board meetings, and the process is more likely to be influenced by personal contacts.

Foundations generally like to initiate, and do not like to pick up after the government. So if you are considering sequential funding, go to the foundations first. On the other hand, all funding sources respond well to multiple funding, in which the project is divided into discrete parts that can be separately funded. Successful funding of any of those parts enhances the chances for the others. Funding agencies also appreciate willingness in the applicant agency to carry some of the cost of a project through grantee contributions. Contributions in the form of matching funds are often *required*.

Sources of Information

Information on foundation sources is available to the extent that the foundations make it available and from reports to the Internal Revenue Service. The information appears in several major directories in which foundations are grouped by their geographic areas (state), by the subject matter of their funding programs, by the recipients, and by the topic areas of past funding.

The best source for research on foundations is the Foundation Center Cooperating Collections Network, called the Foundation Center. This is an independent national service organization established by foundations.

TABLE 2.3
Foundations

Major Types of Foundation by Income Source	Types of Foundation by Funding Interests	Non-operating	Operating
I. Private and Independent Foundations Non-governmental, nonprofit, with funds and programs managed by their own trustees or directors; activities serve the common welfare. All tax exempt foundations are treated as private unless they apply for public status.	1. General Purpose Few restrictions; they like problems with national scope impact, pilot or demonstration projects with high visibility. May have own priorities from year to year; may specialize. E,g.: Rockefeller, Carnegie, Ford, Kellog. 2. Special Purpose Restricted to subject, area or activity in which it is designed to operate. E.g.: Robert Wood Johnson. 3. Family Set up by donor to reflect personal interests; may designate type of recipient, such as college, hospital, community fund. 4. Company Sponsored Endowment and annual contributions from a profit-making corporation. Legally separate; tend to be local-community oriented.	Primary activity is to make grants. A source of funds.	Uses resources to conduct research or provide a service. A recipient of funds. To receive foundation funds an agency must be a private, operating foundation or a public foundation.
II. Public Foundations Supported or operated For the benefit of the public. Substantial amount of support comes from the general public, government, foundation grants; includes categories: churches, educational institutions, hospitals and providers of health care, education, research; government.	5. Community Joint small-scale funds, publicly supported; programs serve local needs; may support ongoing operations of local worth; classed as public charities. 6. Federal Government E.g.: Nat. Sci. Foundation Nat. Endowment for the Arts		

The Center's 173 locations cover the 50 states, Australia, Canada, England, Japan, Mexico, Puerto Rico, and the Virgin Islands. Most house collections of reference materials on foundation giving are located in local libraries. Four, in Washington, D.C.; New York; Cleveland; and San Francisco, are full-service collections operated by the Center.

The national office and main Center branch is located at 79 Fifth Avenue, New York City (212-620-4230). The Center is the publisher of many of the important references on foundation grant giving and will send you a list of the Foundation Center locations. (For an excellent guide to using the Foundation Center, see *Foundation Fundamentals,* in the Selected Bibliography.)

A key reference document is *The Foundation Directory* and *Supplement*. This reports on the 5,000 or more major foundations and gives the most useful information on grant policies and how to apply. The *Supplement* updates the entries and is published one year after each edition of the *Directory*. Other major sources of information, reflecting primarily the topic areas in which foundations have given funding in the past, are the *Foundation Grants Index* and the *COMSEARCH Printouts,* the latter providing past computer searches by geographic or subject area. You can also order a new search for a fee.

The *Foundation Directory* has entries listed as shown in Exhibit 5. If you are looking for a likely prospect, you have several indexes to consult. The Geographic Index lists the states in which foundations are located and then the foundations, with summary information. The drawback to the index is that although a foundation may award grants throughout the nation, it is listed under the state where it is headquartered. This makes it hard to spot if you aren't looking in that particular state. More useful would be a geographic listing by the states of the recipients, with foundations that give nationally listed as such separately. The Geographic Index is most useful when you are in a state with few foundations and your project is not likely to attract a foundation with national recipients. Then there is no problem in reviewing each listing and selecting the ones that appear to fit.

"Donors, Officers, and Trustees" and "Types of Support" are other specialized indexes, but the Subject Index is the most useful. Using relevant topic listings, you get the numbers of the foundations that seem likely; you then examine the main entry in the Foundation Index, where the foundations are listed by number. (Actually, the numbers result in foundation presentation in alphabetical order, state by state.)

The Subject Index would list entries under, for example, cultural programs, higher education, emergency services, and infant care. In the

EXHIBIT 5
Entries in the *Foundation   Directory*

Entry Number (You look up the foundation by numerical order once you find it in an index.)

Foundation Name

Current Address and Phone Number

Date of Incorporation

Donors

Financial Data: Year-end date of the accounting period; assets; gifts received; expenditures: total, number of grants, high award, low award, average award, information on matching gifts; awards to individuals; and loans made — if applicable. (Gives an idea of capacity.)

Purposes and Activities: Example: Grants for higher education including medical education, research, and children's education. (Might specify the geographic area of recipients.)

Types of Support: Example: General purpose, seed money grants, professorships, and special projects.

Limitations: Example: No grants to individuals, nor for capital funds, endowments, or loans. (Geographical limits may be specified.)

Publications: Lists documents like annual reports, application guidelines available to the applicant.

Application Information: Initial approach; deadlines; board meeting dates; final notification; write (person to contact and address application to).

Officers

Trustees

Number of Staff

Employer Identification Number (IRS identification used to look up returns)

main entry you would first check the foundation's "Purposes and Activities" to make sure that what you want to do is covered. Then you check "Limitations" to make sure you are not excluded by activity, location, or any other specific. A check on "Types of Support" lets you know whether the type of help you need is covered.

You look at "Application Information and Publications" to see what you have to do to get funded, the time frame, whom to contact, and how. "Number of Staff" gives you an idea of whether you will be able to make phone inquiries, and the identification number will help should you wish to examine the foundation's IRS returns (990-AR) to see something of recent funding activity.

Once you are armed with a list of potential foundations, you refine your information. You check the *Supplement* to note changes. The next place to look would be the *Source Book Profiles, COMSEARCH Printouts,* or *The Foundation Grants Index.* These list descriptions of awards made by the foundations, the amounts, and the recipients.

One might not wish to start with these, because the point is to find a foundation that matches your interests, and not an award that exactly matches your project. Once you have the foundation, you want to be sure that the awards given are related, but one would never wish to find an actual duplication. However, having the past recipients' names provides information you can use for later networking, since some grant writers consider contact with former recipients one of the best ways to prepare for grant writing. This is mentioned again in Chapter 3.

Examples of Foundation Finding

Example 2: Ambulance Staff Training in Emergency Medical Services

For this example you would be looking for a foundation listed under health, interested in effective medical care delivery, perhaps for heart disease or emergency services. The foundation should be interested in your region or should not be geographically restricted. It should not exclude staff training.

Example 3: City Children Involved in the Arts Community

For this you should find a foundation contributing in your area that gives to social services and cultural organizations. It should permit payment to the artists and perhaps have funds for operating budgets or continuing support. It might offer matching funds to go with your federal grant prospect. If it were interested in promotion of the arts in the community and especially among disadvantaged children, that would be a good fit.

Example 4: Writing Skills for Retention of Graduate Students

With this example you are looking for a foundation that gives to institutions of graduate higher education, public or private, depending on your school. It might be interested in promoting minority graduate education. It should be willing to grant money for curriculum development (beyond normal curriculum development paid for from regular budgets) and perhaps pay for professorships or staff positions.

Example 5: Development of Leadership by Women of Color in the Antiviolence Movement

In this case you would look for a foundation supporting minorities, especially professionals, and social service agencies. It may have given funds to promote leadership training before, or it may be interested in the development of models for leadership training. You could also look for foundations involved with women's issues or family violence.

Other Sources

The *National Data Book* lists over 25,000 active grant-making foundations in the United States, most of which are too small for inclusion in the *Foundation Directory*. State and local directories are available listing foundations and other grant makers by region. Some publishers offer directories by foundation type, area, and/or subject. Specialized directories list funding sources for aging, health, religious activities, higher education, nursing, and the handicapped. In addition there is the Foundation Center's *Foundation Grants to Individuals*. (See the bibliography for a selection of directories.)

For announcements about new foundations and policy changes too new to be included in annual directories, look for public statements reported in the press and monthly updates of some of the major directories.

Once you have found one or two likely sources of funds, there is nothing more important than information from the foundation's own literature and phone contact with its staff.

CORPORATIONS

Corporations make contributions to nonprofit organizations through two major types of structures: "corporate foundations," established separately from the corporation (see Table 2.3), and programs operated within the company under contributions officers. Some do both. A corporate foundation can be treated like any other foundation. But in-house corporate giving has its own set of characteristics and is the newest focus of the literature on grant writing.

Corporate giving can be referred to as corporate charities, corporate contributions, corporate giving programs, or deductible contributions. (Contributions to social programs and organizations can be classed as business expenses.)

With few exceptions, corporations are still not a good source of large amounts of money. They provide little competitive structure and rarely give over $5,000. Corporate giving in 1987 did not increase over 1986 levels, even though overall charitable giving rose 6.5 percent.

Aside from corporate foundations, which are just like other foundations, corporations have little incentive to provide grant money. They are allowed by law to write off 10 percent of pretax profits for tax purposes, but as late as 1986, corporations had not gone over 2 percent. Changes in the tax structure, mergers, acquisitions, leveraged buyouts, divestitures, and scaling down resulted in shrinking company budgets and staff.

However, once funded, a recipient agency can often expect to come back year after year. Sometimes the funds can be used for general operations. When corporations do give, they offer a less formal environment. Personal contacts can be a decisive factor in corporate giving, since corporations are less accountable for their giving decisions.

Corporations prefer to give to a narrow set of recipients: these include higher education, federated giving (like the United Way), and nonprofit agencies in cities where they are headquartered or have major plants. They give for issues of significance to the consumers they serve, to programs that afford visibility, and to projects that promote the corporate image or morale.

Corporations prefer to give in the following ways:

1. Research to supply a segment of knowledge not being carried out inhouse

2. Programs or institutions which can benefit their employees, such as
    a. graduate schools, training programs, special courses
    b. employee assistance programs on drugs, alcohol abuse, smoking, exercise, diet, communication skills; resources development, recreational or cultural facilities
    c. health screening
    d. transportation
    e. programs to improve quality of life
    f. programs dealing with ecological issues

3. Interests of the executive in charge of corporate giving

Corporations make their gifts in the following forms, most of which are not financial:

1. Financial gifts
2. Contributions in kind, such as
    a. use of printing, mailing, computer, transportation facilities in off-hours
    b. assistance with advertising, coop purchasing, loans, repairs, and the loan of the expertise of specialists such as technicians, lawyers, and auditors
    c. loans of equipment
    d. donations of used or excess supplies and products
    e. use of facilities (such as staff dining rooms, conference rooms) for meetings, classes, fund-raising events
    f. hosting of fund-raising events to introduce important potential donors

Sources of Information

New *corporate-giving directories* are increasingly available. Some of these are presented in the bibliography. The grant writer needs several types of directory information. National, state, and local corporate-giving directories list the corporations and information about corporate giving practices. These can be used in a manner similar to the foundation directories and are useful in finding major corporate givers. (Be sure to distinguish corporate foundations from corporate giving programs.)

General corporate directories are national or regional directories of corporations and give general corporate information such as officers, directors, assets, annual revenues, number of employees, financial standing, and location of main offices and plants. *Standard and Poors Register of Corporations* is an example. These directories can be very useful in locating corporations of special interest to you. For example, a producer of video cassette cameras and recorders might be interested in supporting a training program with classes recorded on videotape. A manufacturer of emergency equipment might be interested in a program to deliver a new drug as part of an emergency medical service.

There are local directories that are very useful for locating major corporations in a particular state, town, or county. Once you know the nature of your project, it is useful to consider what kind of corporation would be interested. For example, a senior citizens center may be located near restaurants that would be willing to contribute food. A producer of physical therapy equipment may be willing to supply equipment to a college-based program in physical therapy.

When a corporation is not listed with information about its giving policy, it is best to use the directories to learn the name of the officer you need to reach. Unless the listing advises otherwise, it is fastest to use the telephone, calling the corporate phone number listed, to contact an officer at the senior level.

The key to corporate funding is to find the way your program can best advance the interests of the corporation and communicate this. With few exceptions, corporations only require informal applications, such as a letter. A letter of inquiry could be taken as a proposal, so written communication should be delayed until you know what is involved.

Examples of Corporation Finding

Example 1: Education for Parents of Infants Discharged from Intensive Care

You determine from the local college video arts department the type of equipment needed to tape the parent training sessions and who makes it. You also determine the number of VCRs you need for use in playing the tapes and get the name of the local agency that would be used to duplicate the tapes for in-house use and for distribution. Then you research the companies.

Using the national and local corporate giving directories, you see if there is a record of grants-in-kind, that is, whether the corporations make gifts of their products (or make loans or gifts of used products). You also note the directors of corporate giving. If you are not successful in finding the information you need, you could use general corporate directories to ascertain the names of the contact persons to reach.

Example 3: City Children Involved in the Arts Community

You might get a list of local art suppliers, costumers, and shops that handle the materials and equipment to be used in the sessions with the students. These firms could be asked to contribute these supplies for the project, or at least offer a substantial discount. These contributions and discounts would count as matching funds.

You or your colleagues may question putting your program in the hands of executives who have their own priorities and are not really accountable to the public or stockholders, but a meeting with the director of corporate giving is not the time or place to express such qualms. So consult early with your agency people about their views.

3

The Process of Finding Funding

FINDING PROSPECTS

Now that you have an orientation about funding agencies, you can consider the sequence of events in actual grant development. Assuming that you have had the preliminary meetings with your agency people discussed in Chapter 1, it would now be a good idea to write a brief project description, similar to the examples presented in Exhibit 1.

Armed with the description, your task is to find several funding agencies with interests and constraints that match your project idea. Grant getting is really about *giving grantors what they want.* You are looking for grantors who want to fund what you want to do. That is matchmaking.

You may wish to consider which are the most logical types of funding agencies. A project to examine occupational disease rates and exposure to toxic chemicals will have a different kind of funder from a project to teach orthodox religious practices in a parochial day-care center. The normal sources are the federal government, state agencies, foundations, and corporations. But you may also find it fruitful to consider trade unions (which have funds for member services and education and are interested in safety and health), local community groups, and individual contributors. You can also think about alternatives to grant getting such as revenues from sales.

Another consideration is whether you have some leads you can immediately investigate, such as funding agencies that are providing current funding or that have provided past funding. They may be willing to go on to a next stage of funding or to explore new avenues, especially if you have had a good track record so far. Former refusals may be promising if the agencies left the door open to later approaches; more so if the original refusal was based on a temporary lack of funds or a mismatch of interests.

MAKING A PRELIMINARY MATCH

Early on, you should list all the possible ways your idea might be indexed. Think of headings to represent the problem, the discipline, the target population's demographic characteristics, the type of agency you represent, the region, the type of setting, such as urban or rural, and any other such descriptors. Another way is to read the indexes and note the topics that may apply to you. Knowing the possible categories helps you utilize the indexes and the available computer searches for the *Catalog of Federal Domestic Assistance* and COMSEARCH, available at the Foundation Center in your area. (As an old-fashioned academic, this author prefers to get the "feel" of indexes by personal inspection, not relatively blind computer selection.)

Using the sources discussed in Chapter 2, you collect a list of several potential funding agencies. Then you go more deeply into a review of their pattern of giving, the size of their past awards, and their application procedures. You then examine your mutual compatibility.

1. Does the funding agency have the same interests, intentions, and concerns as you and your agency? Examine the material available on the funding agency's mission and policies. Examine your own agency's goals. Is there a clear and obvious relationship between the proposed project, the funding agency's interests, and your agency's interests?

2. Can you formulate your program in terms of the guidelines and priorities of the funding agency, but not to the detriment or distortion of your own? Is it still the project you had in mind? Better? Worse? Are you willing to change?

3. Does the funding agency make grants in amounts reasonably close to the amount you need for the project? Examine directory information, IRS and annual reports.

4. If the agency has regular start-up dates for recipients, is the date you can expect to start compatible with your needs?

5. Do you conform to the special requirements set by the funding agency? That is, do you fit within any limits set on the following:

a. Appropriate target population. Demographic or ethnic characteristics.
b. Type of service or activity. Don't confuse basic research with social service, for example.
c. Type of institution. Government, individual, nonprofit, for profit.
d. Goals. What purpose do you share?
e. Location. Is there a particular geographic target?
f. Credentials of staff members. Are there professional or credential requirements for the staff?
g. Obligations to carry out specific activities. These may include a treatment protocol, work with other agencies, or adherence to fiscal reporting procedures.
h. Financial requirements. Matching funds/grantee contributions.

MAKING CONTACT

Once you have some tentative matches, your indispensable next step is to phone for the agency's literature, guidelines, and application materials. They provide much more specific information; you may find that you do not have a fit after all. You obtain addresses, names, and titles of people to contact from the directories discussed in Chapter 2. Note whether the agency responds to preliminary proposals or encourages an initial interview.

Making initial contact is best by phone. You can arrange to receive the applications and guidelines, ask about the latest deadlines (they are often shifted), and check out questions you might have about what you have read so far. If you find that you must write to obtain the application information, be sure that the letter cannot be interpreted as an application.

Make informal personal contact with the funding agency. Even when there is only a national office name listed in the *Catalog*, the application materials will list regional staff offices and names of people to whom you can address your questions. Such persons can give you some indication of whether the agency would be interested in your proposal and will be there for you as you continue with the grant writing.

During the grant-writing stage, it is very helpful to have personal phone contact with the staff in a federal agency or a large foundation. These professionals can help you interpret ambiguous instructions, give you tips on what is wanted, and provide suggestions for future funding.

It is important to learn how to cultivate a working relationship with funding agency staff members. (A National Science Foundation survey of 14,000 principal investigators revealed that investigators who contacted NSF staff personally or in writing before submitting a proposal were somewhat more likely to get funding.)

Make contact with someone who has been funded by the agency. You may already know someone who has had such funding, or you may find someone by using the directories mentioned in Chapter 2. Talk about the experience of applying and succeeding; agencies have different styles of functioning. Such a contact can help you assess the relative importance of various topics presented in this book.

SOME PRACTICAL TIPS

Use a preliminary "discussion paper" as a basis for phone exploration of whether an agency is appropriate for you. You can then also use it for a letter of inquiry and to promote support within your agency or among the target population. See the suggested outline later in this chapter.

Never give a clerical person so much information that he or she makes a decision about whether your project is fundable. Accept such a judgment only from someone in authority. On the other hand, respect the clerical staff, because they can have an influence on how you are received.

When attempting to speak to funding project managers, consider that they are busy people. Make appointments for phone interviews; always ask if they have time to talk before starting a conversation. Always end with an understanding of the next step and who is to do what. Be clear. Keep notes on conversations so as not to forget commitments.

If you are encouraged to write a letter to a foundation or corporation to determine whether they would be interested in your proposal, be very careful to avoid having the letter of inquiry mistaken for an application. Some agencies have so few application requirements that a one-page letter might be treated as an application. You could be rejected before you have made a case.

FEDERAL REVIEW: EXECUTIVE ORDER 12372, INTERGOVERNMENTAL REVIEW

This refers to the federal government's system requiring review by state and local governments of grant applications for selected grant programs. Each state has been required to design its own review process and selects the programs for which it wishes to review applications. Applications must meet the requirements of a given state's review processes before the federal agencies take action. The process was designed to allow state and local *objections* to surface before federal action is taken; it is not really an endorsement process. Even after federal approval, a state may ask for modifications or an explanation from the federal granting agency.

Some states' procedures do not require early notification of intent. Only approved preapplications are of interest, and these serve as project notification. A standard federal assistance application form has a place to indicate that a "Notification of Intent" and a review process apply.

Once the preapplication is approved, if Executive Order 12372, "Intergovernmental Review of Federal Programs," applies, a state usually requires advance copies of the final proposal. Therefore, early preparation is wise, to allow time to respond to any objections or inquiries from state and local agencies.

The federal agency will be able to tell you whether intergovernmental review is required; the application packet should have the specific forms and list the necessary steps for E.O. 12372 if it applies. The *Catalog of Federal Domestic Assistance* refers to the process in the program descriptions and has an appendix that shows a checkmark if your funding agency's program is covered by requirements for intergovernmental review.

HEALTH SYSTEMS AGENCY REVIEW

Health systems agencies (HSAs) have been responsible for the review and approval of health facilities and programs, including proposals for new construction and proposed changes of existing facilities. Such programs, if federally funded, have been subject to "project review," including public hearings. New programs affecting patient welfare are usually subject to "appropriateness review," and are not subject to public hearings. That is the kind of program you would be likely to seek funding to do.

Since the fiscal 1987 federal budget, HSAs are dependent on state funds. While some state HSAs were funded, it is unlikely that project review for most projects will be carried out. In the past HSA has waived its right to review many direct care, educational, and all research programs. HSA can be helpful in indicating where an idea fits into the regional priorities of the HSA Master Plan.

PRELIMINARY DISCUSSION PAPER

A preliminary discussion paper would help you to articulate what you have in mind to get funded. It provides a reference that can be copied, disseminated, and referred to in discussions with others who will be involved in the planning process. It can also serve as a basis for your introduction in the proposal. One page is enough.

You cover what the program will do, whom it will serve, and what agency is to carry it out. You also pinpoint just what it is in the funding agency's program that your project idea addresses. The paper focuses on the *activities* for which you want funding. It is only a first statement about activities to be undertaken, and it is subject to change. Also, it will be somewhat different for each funding agency, reflecting that agency's requirements, interests and constraints.

The one-page paper should answer the following questions:

1. What is the main activity of this project; what will it do?

2. What population will be served; the target population? (Describe its location, numbers, and characteristics.)

3. What agency is applying for funds? (Give your agency's name, type, function, location.)

4. What is the funding agency, and which of its programs do you address?

5. How do you qualify?

6. What is the type of program? For example, the program may be a
    a. *needs assessment,* to determine conditions in the target population or intellectual or academic discipline.
    b. *planning grant,* to organize an approach and design a major undertaking, which will be followed later by program implementation.
    c. *research grant,* to add to pure or applied knowledge in a discipline. (State hypothesis.)
    d. *pilot study,* to find initial indicators that the method will work and to identify potential problems.
    e. *demonstration project,* to show that a known methodology can be successfully adapted to a new location or population group.
    f. *clinical trial,* to test a specific treatment for a specific target population compared with an alternative and/or a placebo.

> g. *program trial,* to test a specific method for a given target population compared with an alternative and/or no program.

Item 6 can become a one-sentence description of the project, designed to place the project in the context of the granting agency's grant categories. The following are examples.

a.　The project is a *needs assessment study* to learn the perceived social service needs, utilization levels and patterns, and the health/belief system of members of the Caribbean community in _____ City.

b.　The project is a *planning study* to design and win support for a city-wide consortium of schools, hospitals, and other health-related facilities and the scientific community — to provide the latest AIDS prevention, education, counseling, and treatment techniques — for later implementation in a coordinated service program.

c.　The project is a *research study* to measure the labor-force participation effect of providing free day care to welfare mothers.

d.　The project is a *pilot study* to explore how homeless families respond to living in small-cluster housing units where day care is provided.

e.　The project is a *demonstration study* to show that junior- and senior-year participation in a series of career explorations and summer internships can increase the number of minority students applying for postsecondary training in the helping professions.

f.　The project is a *clinical trial* of a new treatment for Stage I and II breast cancer among women ages 20 to 70, compared with a conventional treatment alternative.

g.　The project is a *program trial* comparing the effectiveness of exercise and diet-modification education with medication for the reduction of serum cholesterol among members of a community center.

PLANNING

Once you are clear on where you want to apply for funds, the next steps involve planning. This section helps you get yourself organized for the work of grant writing.

Funding Time Plan: Funding Agency Requirements

1. You start by having a time frame within which you commit yourself and a set of requirements you must meet. These come from the funding agency. Check the accuracy of your current information:
   a. Is the program still in existence?
   b. Do funds still exist?
   c. Are the mutual interests between your agency and the funding agency still in effect?
   d. Are your guidelines and application forms the latest?
   e. Are your deadline dates for the preapplication and/or application the most recent?
   f. If there are no actual deadline dates, or if the period is long, does the agency advise submitting early or late in the fiscal year? Well before or at the deadline date?

2. Make sure you know the time frame for the application procedure(s) and what you have to do.
   a. What is the review period and when can you expect to hear the reply for both the preapplication and a final proposal? How long between preapplication approval and the deadline for submitting the final proposal?
   b. Can you expect to meet with the funding agency for feedback during any of these periods? Do they like site visits?
   c. If interviews are permitted, is it best to make appointments by phone and/or by letter?

3. Check with people in your agency. Discuss the funding-agency deadlines, restrictions, and other items listed above. Find out if there are people in your agency and board who have contacts at the funding agency. Consider whether you can legitimately draw on these contacts to support your proposal or provide guidance.

4. Note whether Intergovernmental Review or Health Systems Agency Review, described earlier, will be required. If so, note the "single point of contact" given for your state and make contact.

5. The regional HSA can be helpful in showing where an idea fits into its long-range plans. (Note that this agency may no longer be in existence when you read this, since each HSA's continued existence has been put under state control.) HSAs will probably ask for notification only after a preapplication has been accepted, but it is a good idea to make contact early.

6. Meet with or call potential clientele, experts, policymakers, and interested groups to ask for comments, suggestions, criticisms, advice, and potential support for the proposed project.

7. Consider the time needed to prepare the applications; meet with your agency people; get endorsements and letters of support; edit and retype; and go through the final review process, including intergovernmental review. Can you meet the deadlines? Should you choose a later funding cycle?

4

Preparation for Writing

OUTLINES

This section presents a framework for writing grant proposals. In the vast array of proposal application forms and guidelines, no two are alike, and the grant writer has to read each set of instructions carefully each time an attempt is made to get funding. But there is an implicit order.

This book offers a general outline and sections on writing that cover almost any conceptual category required by an application. While the order of presentation of the subject matter may vary, if the grant writer has mastered the ideas underlying each section and their interrelationships, the general outline presented here can be adapted to any order of presentation required. And if fewer subjects are called for than those presented here, the others can be included as subcategories, provided there is space. Sometimes material not called for can enhance a presentation.

Table 4.1 presents the generic outline of this book on the left in parts A and B of the table. On the right in part A there are two examples summarized from federal agency guidelines. Part B repeats the generic outline and offers examples summarizing two foundation outlines. The reader will note by following the letters and numbers in the examples that the outlines differ in order of presentation and in language. But the similarity of ideas is evident. Some terms like "Problem/Need Statement" do not appear in research proposals, where the term "Rationale" is often used. The term "Research Design" can replace the term "Methods." Most foundations do not have application forms, and some do not even specify what is to be covered. In these cases the generic outline can be used with ease.

TABLE 4.1

Comparison of Proposal Outlines

Part A: Generic and Federal Outlines

Generic Outline	Sample Federal Outline 1.	Sample Federal Outline 2.

LETTER OF TRANSMITTAL
  Tells funder what is en-
  closed/program addressed.
	LETTER OF TRANSMITTAL:
	  No./title of priority
	  subject area addressed.
		1. APPLICANT ORGANIZATION
		2. CATEGORY OF SUPPORT
		3. PERIOD OF SUPPORT

SUMMARY
  Abstract covering major
  sections of proposal.
	ABSTRACT
	  Up to 2 pages, w/o
	  giving project period.
		4. SUMMARY OF PROJECT
		5. NO. PERSONS EXPECTED TO
		   BENEFIT (AUDIENCE/STUDENTS)

INTRODUCTION
  Introduces sponsor, proj-
  ect; which part of fund-
  er's program addressed.
	INTRODUCTION includes
	  geographic location of
	  areas to be served;
	  maps go to appendix.
		A. PRESENT ORGANIZATION, TITLE
		   OF PROJECT, FUNCTION
		B. DIRECTOR

NEED/PROBLEM STATEMENT
  Main problem; contribut-
  ing and intermediary
  problems address; docu-
  mented by local and in-
  stitutional data/proofs.
	A. PROBLEM; B. CONTRIBUTING
	   FACTORS. Health status
	   problems addressed and
	   contributing problems;
	   how latter will affect
	   general problem.
		D. EVIDENCE OF NEED

OBJECTIVES
  Long range goals; project
  results matched to prob-
  lems; expected outcomes.
	C. GOALS; D. OUTCOME OBJEC-
	   TIVES. Use the indices
	   of baseline data in
	   problems; other results.
		C. PRINCIPAL OBJECTIVES

METHODS (PROGRAM)
  How each objective will
  be accomplished, includ-
  ing products.
	E. METHODOLOGY
	   Plan of action/activi-
	   ties; target population
	   staffing; features such
		E. METHODS OF IMPLEMENTATION

SIGNIFICANCE OF METHODS
  Why methods were chosen
  given state of the art.
	as technology, costs,
	   lit. review and reasons
	   for selecting methods.
		G. NEW STAFF POSITIONS IF ANY

EVALUATION DESIGN
  How each objective will
  be assessed; success cri-
  teria/research methods.
	F. TRACKING OF PROJECT IM-
	   PLEMENTATION Activity
	   schedule/controls.
	G. MONITORING/EVALUATION
		F. METHODS OF EVALUATION

LEVEL/EFFORT; PLAN OF WORK
  Plan of operations; re-
  sources needed.
	Describe data to be
	   collected; success cri-
	   teria, evaluation meth-
		PROGRAMMING PLANNED

SIGNIFICANCE: IMPACT/RESULTS
  Benefits of project be-
  yond immediate sponsor.
	odology and analysis.
	H. USE OF PROJECT INFO.
	   How news of progress	

SPONSORSHIP, ORG. CAPABILITY
  Support by sponsor; evi-
  dence of capability to
  carry out the project.
	will be disseminated; to
	   whom; ways that others
	   will benefit.
	I. CAPABILITIES OF APPLI-
		LIST OF PRIOR GRANTS;
		SIGNED, AUDITED FINANCIAL
		STATEMENT; REVENUES/EXPENS.
		HISTORY OF ORGANIZATION;

SUPPORT AND ENDORSEMENT
  Evidence that project is
  approved by others.
	CANT. Past accomplish-
	   ments/funding. People
	   and organizations to be
		STATEMENT OF PURPOSE
		
		LETTERS OF SUPPORT

FUTURE FUNDING NEEDS
  Proof of eventual self-
  sufficiency.
	involved; credentials/
	   duties.	

BUDGET; JUSTIFICATIONS
  Budget detail and explan-
  ation of major items.
	J. BUDGET/JUSTIFICATION
	   For each item/activity.
		BUDGET, INCLUDING MATCHING
		FUNDS

APPENDED MATERIALS	Vitae for key people.	BIOGRAPHIES

continued

TABLE 4.1, continued

Part B: Generic and Foundation Outlines

Generic Outline	Foundation Outline 1.	Foundation Outline 2.
LETTER OF TRANSMITTAL Tells funder what is en- closed/program addressed.	COVER LETTER	1. COVER LETTER. What is re- quested; objectives; sig- nificance; major
SUMMARY Abstract covering major sections of proposal.	SUMMARY, including amount requested, total budget, grant purpose, expected	activities to be carried out.
INTRODUCTION Introduces sponsor, proj- ect; which part of fund-	results. INTRODUCTION. Includes	
er's program addressed.	1. Amount requested.	
NEED/PROBLEM STATEMENT Main problem; contribut- ing and intermediary problems address; docu- mented by local and in- stitutional data/proofs.	2. NEED OR PROBLEM; simi- lar programs and their performance.	2. PROPOSAL
OBJECTIVES Long range goals; project results matched to prob- lems; expected outcomes.	3. OBJECTIVES. How the need will be met or the problem addressed by the project.	a. Detailed description of program design; what is to be accomplished.
METHODS (PROGRAM) How each objective will be accomplished, includ- ing products.	4. Target population/group who will benefit. Demo- graphic/geographic in- formation.	
SIGNIFICANCE OF METHODS Why methods were chosen given state of the art.	5. Timetable for conduct of program, incl. start and termination dates.	
EVALUATION DESIGN How each objective will be assessed; success cri- teria/research methods.	9. How and when success will be measured.	b. How project will be evaluated.
LEVEL/EFFORT;PLAN OF WORK Plan of operations; re- sources needed.		
SIGNIFICANCE:IMPACT/RESULTS Benefits of project be- yond immediate sponsor.		
SPONSORSHIP, ORG.CAPABILITY Support by sponsor; evi- dence of capability to carry out the project.	6. Staff qualifications/ duties/time. 7. Why sponsor is appro- priate to carry out	c. Qualifications or capa- bilities of organization
SUPPORT AND ENDORSEMENT Evidence that project is approved by others.	program; history. 8. Board members info. 11. Other sources con-	
FUTURE FUNDING NEEDS Proof of eventual self- sufficiency.	tacted for funding. 12 Plans for securing future financial	
BUDGET; JUSTIFICATIONS Budget detail and explan- ation of major items.	support, if needed. 10. Detailed Budget	d. Budget, including antici- pated expenditures, income, and sources.
APPENDED MATERIALS	13. Current organizational fiscal information.	3. ORGANIZATIONAL INFORMATION.

A further area for consideration is the length of the applications. When a federal application asks for no more than 2 pages for the summary, 35 pages for the narrative, and 50 for appendix material, as is the case in the first federal example, they really mean it. Additional pages are thrown away, and the instructions in this case say so! Many foundations ask for no more than 5 pages, and some federal preapplications ask for only 5.

In the case of RFPs for research *contracts,* the RFP will present a statement of need and scope of work in much detail. The offerer is expected to take these and, particularly in the scope of work, carry them forward into a much more detailed and advanced description of the activities to be carried out. The language of the proposal is expected to be sophisticated and reflect knowledge of the field.

The RFP may include an outline of the projected narrative, covering the scope of work or study design, staff, organizational capabilities, administration, and budget or costs. Sometimes the activities called for are referred to as *tasks*; and tangible results may be called *products.* You are usually allowed to add additional tasks or products, and you may wish to budget them separately.

Items in a scope of work may include

A requirement to furnish personnel, materials, and equipment necessary to develop and deliver a product, report, or the like

Steps required to accomplish the above, including, sometimes, the subjects to be covered and the institutions or data bases to be dealt with

Related services to be provided, and to whom

Additional data to be collected

Products to be produced

Further specifications

Related problems to be addressed

WORKING WITH THE APPLICATION FORMS AND GUIDELINES

Assuming that you have received the application forms and guidelines from the federal agency and/or foundation, the steps presented here are a guide to how to make the best use of them.

1. Study each set of forms. Read the instructions and guidelines carefully. Make notes on the sections required for the proposal and the preapplication if there is a preapplication phase. Note the differences.

2. Copy all application forms; store the originals for final typing.

3. Use the generic outline and see where each of the topics appears in the funder's outline. Identify the funder's terms if they are different from those in the generic, and compare the meanings by reading the funder's instructions. Use the funding agency's terms, but know what they refer to in this book. Where the funding agency does not include a counterpart for a section of the generic outline, consider whether it will enhance your proposal and find where in the funder's outline you can include it.

4. From the request for proposal, application form, or guidelines, identify the *criteria* the agency will use in selecting projects for funding. Use the criteria in planning how you will present such material as the problem/needs statement, objectives, method, evaluation design, significance, and organizational capability. If it is not obvious how to do this, consider adding topics to the outline to cover the criteria as specifically as possible. Table 4.2 presents a summary of sample criteria, some excerpted from much longer lists.

5. If Intergovernmental Review or HSA review is required, make sure you know whether the funding agency's outline will be acceptable. If not, obtain the review agency's forms early so you can write a proposal to satisfy all the outlines. You do this by developing an outline that includes *all* the topics asked for by *any* agency and using multitopic headings in your document where there are equivalencies. Generic outline topics can be included in a similar way.

6. Having created a master outline, it is helpful to create file folders for each outline topic. Then, as you get ideas, you can jot them down and put them in the proper folder. Similarly, as you collect reference material, statistics, and letters of support and/or feedback, you can file them for future use.

7. Lay out a time plan for writing each section and stick with it.

8. Consult the appropriate literature to document need, select and measure objectives, select or compare methods, and ascertain realistic success criteria achieved by others in the field. Prepare the bibliography that you will draw on for this. Consider the theoretical literature related to the problem and reports of programs already funded in the field. See, for example, the bibliography of final reports of government-funded programs collected by the National Technical Information Service (NTIS). Consider, too, evaluation reports in the journals of the field.

TABLE 4.2
Examples of Criteria Used to Review Applications

FEDERAL GRANT	FEDERAL GRANT	FOUNDATION	FOUNDATION
PRIORITIES/CRITERIA Maternal and Infant Health: VI Emerging Issues in M & I H. of regional/national significance; vulner- able population: spe- cific service. Justification; not covered in other areas and not replication of work already done. NARRATIVE Rationale justifying need for project. 1.Problem: identified, range of character- istics/consequences shown for nation, project pop., area, minority groups/area. Shows links between the broad and related problems addressed. Describes measurements for health status; problems specified, justified, practical. Baseline data in target population or plan to obtain it early in project provided. 2.Contributing Factors Review of Literature. Supports: link to main problem with data. States: which will be addressed. 3.Outcome Objectives Identifies time frame Measurable objectives for each goal. Uses same indices as with problems. Evidence:objectives are feasible in time frame. (Partial list of criteria)	CRITERIA Merit of Project/ Service. -Applicant able to help presenters demonstrate cre- ative leadership in programing, ability to attract broader audiences. -Evidence of clear, achievable objec- tives for project. -Evidence methods can be effective. -Evidence need for project in rela- tion to other resources. -Evidence of proper budgeting. Organizational Capabilities -Evidence appropri- ate staff/exper- tise for project. -Organizational stability, fiscal responsibility. Involvement of Presenters -Evidence that pre- senters were rep- resented in plan- ning for project. Dissemination of Results -Applicant's abil- ity to disseminate results nationally or regionally; evidence in budget and plan of work. -Plans should not require continued Endowment funding.	REVIEW 1.Project's rele- vance to Founda- tion's priorities and objectives. 2.Qualifications/ training of proj- ect director and personnel. 3.Capacity to achieve project objectives. 4.Budget by line items. 5.Site visit report if applicable. 6.Availability or duplication of similar program or services in the same geogra- phic area. 7.Number of persons to be reached in target population	CRITERIA a.Organization demonstrates ability to solve problems/provide direct services. b.Innovative pro- gram/broad based community support c.Program encour- ages self-suffi- ciency of parti- cipants. d.Will serve large number of consti- tuents. e.Evidence and prospects of support elsewhere in the community.

THE BASIC COMPONENTS: OVERVIEW

Grant proposals start with *problems*. The underlying assumption is that the applicant agency has selected a significant problem that it is committed to solve. If your agency is a local service agency, you will be focusing on your community's problems. If your agency is a specialty center such as a college department or national treatment center, you will more likely be focusing on advancing the state of the art involved, rather than on the particular community.

The grant proposal offers to help solve the problem with a specific *method* — which is the project's main activity. When the problem is a lack of knowledge, the project tends to be a research proposal; when it addresses the needs of a community, the project tends to be service oriented; and when it deals with a broad negative condition, the project tends to be generic in focus, that is, model building for broad application.

You may note that the preliminary discussion paper focused on the activity that solves the problem, and not the problem itself. It is more usual for the applicant agency to want to deliver a specific program than for it to come up with a new problem it wants to solve. The mission of the applicant agency already delimits the problem areas it addresses, and these are usually taken for granted. However, the danger is that the applicant agency may focus on what it wants to do without sufficient attention to the priorities of its clients or to selection of the best possible method. The proposal framework forces the applicant agency to address such issues.

While it is easier to first write about what you want to do, this was only a way to get you started. Actual grant writing will ask you to think as though you first selected the problem because of its significance, and then selected a method to solve it. You must show that the proposed method is the best one to solve the problem selected.

The *objectives* of the project are the changes in the problem condition you promise to deliver by the end of the project period. Usually the objectives are presented after the problem statement. Once the problem is understood, the method (program) is judged for its ability to achieve the objectives.

You will be funded if your problem is significant, if your objectives are worthwhile, and if your method is considered to be appropriate. Finally, the funding agency will determine whether your agency can be expected to carry out its program effectively.

To prepare for the major writing of the proposal, it is best to first concentrate on the project's problems, objectives, methods, and significance and develop the other sections later. These parts have a logical interrelationship that the following sections will help you perceive.

Before you actually begin to do serious writing, you are invited to read the appendix on style. It can be used as an aid to writing each time you do a section of the proposal.

5

Basic Components of the Proposal: Introduction

The introduction follows the project's title and gets its own section heading. It is the lead-in, to help the reader follow the logic of the proposal. Your discussion paper can be used for the introduction, but you must also include items you cannot cover until you have developed the proposal. Be sure to include the following:

1. The nature of what follows, such as a discussion paper, preapplication, proposal.
2. The specific part of the funder's offering you are addressing.
3. The time period for funding.
4. The total amount required and the amount requested.
5. The main activity; what the project will do and the type of program.
6. The population to be served, the "target population": its location, numbers, and characteristics.
7. The agency applying for funds (your agency name, type, function, location), and how it qualifies.

You might also include some background material, such as why your agency decided to do the project. If there are special features, include them. Be brief, no more than one or two pages.

The introduction is best written after you have done most of the writing; it is easier to be succinct after you have had practice writing about the program. (The author prefers to write a draft introduction, knowing full well it will have to be revised at the end.) The introduction is written as though there were no summary at the beginning, although there usually is. You may repeat parts of the summary if you like the wording.

Examples of proposal introductions appear in Exhibit 6. These examples, as others in the book, are based on the project ideas presented in Exhibit 1. While they may reflect the outlines or guidelines of granting agencies, they do not necessarily correspond to the requirements of any specific funding agency.

EXHIBIT 6
Examples of Proposal Introductions

Example 1: Education for Parents of Infants Discharged from Intensive Care

INTRODUCTION

This is a proposal for a demonstration project to show that infant morbidity and mortality subsequent to discharge from neonatal intensive care units can be reduced through parent education prior to discharge and continued follow-up care by means of infant care clinics and refresher training for parents. The target population will be 300–500 parents of 300 infants discharged from neonatal intensive care units (NICUs) at ____ Hospital Center over a three-year period. The population served includes a high percentage of poverty level and minority mothers and children.

The proposed three-year project addresses the priority area: Maternal and Child Health, Number VI, Emerging Issues in Maternal and Child Health.

Infants discharged from NICUs are at risk for high rates of morbidity, including developmental disabilities, and for mortality. Minority infants and poverty infants, with the highest incidence of the chief risk factor, that of low birth weight, are still at highest risk upon discharge.

Dr. ____, the Chief of Pediatrics at ____ Medical Center, a state hospital, will direct the project, to be sponsored by the ____ Medical Center, located in ____ and serving the city as a whole in its NICU facilities. The Hospital's Patient Education Department, its NICU discharge team, and the nursing faculty of ____ University will be cooperating to produce a series of multilingual, hands-on, videotaped classes and workshop sessions for mothers and other caretakers of the infants.

Training will cover the special caretaking skills needed, how to monitor health and development and how to provide emergency care in life-threatening circumstances. This is expected to make the difference in infant health and survival. An outpatient clinic designed to monitor and care for the NICU graduates will also be instituted.

The first year will cover development of the educational materials, design of the evaluation instruments, provision of clinic services, and the start of the program. The second year will include continuation of the project and the beginning of evaluation analysis after 18 months of infant monitoring. One hundred infants and their parents will be part of the evaluation design, which will follow the infants for 18 months after discharge.

continued

Expected costs for the first year are $____, of which $____ is requested; $____ will be raised by contributions in kind and grantee contributions. Budgets for the second the third years are expected to be $____ and $____, respectively, of which $____ and $____ will be requested.

Example 2: Ambulance Staff Training in Emergency Medical Services

INTRODUCTION

The ____ Hospital Center, a voluntary community hospital located in ____ proposes the following project for consideration by the ____ Foundation. The project addresses the prime interests of the foundation: "The need to support innovations in medical care that can improve care at minimal increased cost" and "to determine the value of specific forms of care by measuring their outcome."

A demonstration project is proposed to show that in-the-field administration by paramedics of streptokinase, a clot-dissolving medication, will significantly reduce the time now required to administer the drug to patients suffering a heart attack and thus improve outcomes, and that this can be done without an increase in the current incidence of adverse effects associated with in-hospital administration of the medication.

The main activities of the project will be (1) preparation of paramedics in the intravenous infusion of streptokinase; (2) monitoring its administration to 50 patients, served by the ____ hospital emergency medical teams, who present in the field with the clinical signs and symptoms of acute myocardial infarction prior to transport to the emergency department of the hospital, and (3) assessment of patient outcomes.

The project is designed to run for one year. Costs for which funding is requested are $____, excluding grantee contributions for equipment and instrumentation. Grantee contributions are estimated at $____ for equipment and instrumentation. This has already been pledged from corporate sources. See Appendix ____.

Example 3: City Children Involved in the Arts Community

INTRODUCTION

The ____ Cooperative Center for the Arts and Education is a nonprofit, tax-exempt organization established to promote audiences for the several arts it represents and to provide opportunities for joint cost sharing and cultural exchange with the community. Located in ____, it serves that unique section of the city housing its resident multimedia artists, called ____. This proposal addresses the stated goals of the ____ Foundation, to promote the well being of the citizens of ____ through increased involvement in the arts of the city's youth.

The proposed pilot project will be run by the center in cooperation with the public elementary school system serving the city. Ten cooperating presenting units — three artists, two photographers, two sculptors, two dance companies, and a theater troupe — will each offer two-hour open sessions once a week for 14 weeks in the fall and spring terms of the school year. Ten student groups of 15 to 20 students in the first

continued

through eighth grades will be taken from the schools located in the central and poverty areas of the city. Assuming that each will participate in five sessions, about 1,000 students will be served during the project year.

The sessions will be work-in-progress, rehearsal, and thinking-out-loud work sessions, in which the artists explore with the students what they are trying to achieve and how they are going about it. Once each term the students will attend finished performances and/or art shows.

The requested funding for one year is $____. Contributions in kind will cover equipment and supplies in the amount of $____. Total budget: $____.

6

Basic Components of the Proposal: Problem/Need

THE BROAD PROBLEM

This description of the *problem/needs statement,* along with the objectives and methods statements in Chapters 7 and 8, is presented as a guide to preparation of your funding proposal. It offers some definitions and a conceptual framework, the terminology of which may not be used everywhere. Remember that the nature of your proposed project determines how relevant this material is. For example, if you propose a classical research project, some of this will not apply.

There are conditions, such as negative health status, premature death, illiteracy, homelessness, suffering, violence, and other negative qualities of life, that are obvious problems that must be solved. These are the real reasons that a project is undertaken. However, such broad problems cannot be solved by single projects funded for one or two years and limited to the scope of a single institution or area. Broad problems generally have complex causes, one or two of which become the focus for individual projects.

Since no one project is able, usually, to address all the causes of a broad problem, you may not always be able to demonstrate changes in the broad problem by the end of the project. Or there may be no change recordable in a short period of time. But you *will* demonstrate changes in the contributing problems you are addressing. For example, you may wish to decrease the rate of lung cancer in your community. Smoking, pollution, diet, heredity, and occupational exposures to asbestos are some of the contributing problems. If you select a smoking cessation program for teenagers, you may be successful in changing smoking rates by the end of the project period, but you cannot expect to see a change in the lung cancer rate by the end of your project, even among teenagers.

Funding agencies expect you to state the broad problem you are addressing with your project. If you plan a program to tell teenagers about careers, or to teach graduate students to write better, or to develop women of color as leaders in antiviolence programs, or to teach paramedicals to administer a new drug, what is the broad problem you are addressing? The ultimate reason?

The broad problems are probably lack of upward career mobility for minority youth, youth unemployment, low entry rates into some professions by the educationally disadvantaged, violence in the home, or mortality rates due to heart disease. Other broad problems might be homeboundness and physical dependency among the physically handicapped, or loneliness among the aged.

WRITING ABOUT THE BROAD PROBLEM

In writing your proposal you describe the broad problem first. You thus provide the ultimate justification for the project, the context within which you later elaborate the specifics your project will address. State the broad problem and provide some statistical or other support to show the significance of the problem nationally. Then specify and document the problem locally and, if you can, in your institution (if that is applicable).

This means introducing the *target population* you will serve. These are the people your institution serves, hopes to attract, or wishes to reach. You state who is affected by the problem, especially if some groups are more affected than others. The target population should be described in terms of geographic location, numbers, and demographics that are relevant to the problem or describe those whom you will serve. (In a pure research project the target population may not be relevant.)

If you expect to show a reduction in the broad problem or a part of it within the time frame of the project, it is a good idea to give *baseline data,* that is, current data for your target population, so you can compare later results with these. Contrast the national with the local incidence of the problem if that is relevant.

If you cannot show the figures for your immediate target population, consider collecting such "needs assessment" data as part of the project. However, it is better to take the time to do a needs assessment before you write the proposal. Reporting such data strengthens your argument that the problem is significant in your locale and establishes your research capability. Such prior research data can convince the funding agency of your seriousness about and commitment to the project.

CONTRIBUTING PROBLEMS

Most broad problems are caused by a complex set of factors. Many such factors are behaviors that are harmful or actions not being taken, whether by individuals, institutions, or governments. These can be thought of as behavioral problems. If your project is designed to change smoking behavior, provide day care, offer police protection, or engage in other activities that will help change the broad problem situation, these indicate your contributing behavioral problems. Other examples: women of color are not making major contributions to program design in family violence projects; patients are not receiving medication soon enough; parents are not administering proper preventive care at home.

In research, the contributing problem can be the need for a certain kind of information, the lack of which is retarding progress in the field. Not knowing the validity of a hypothesis or lacking descriptive data can be contributing problems. (The method is the way the information will be gathered.)

The particular aspects you choose to address, your contributing problems, will reflect the theoretical model you subscribe to. For example, in smoking, a contributor to lung cancer, the target population you choose and the emphasis you take may reflect your belief that smoking by young people is more important to tackle than advertising by the manufacturers of cigarettes. So rather than promoting a ban on advertising, you seek funding for a school-based program to get teenagers to quit or not start smoking. Having made the selection, the choice of method is implied; probably you will choose an educational program, rather than public action, to organize social pressure for legislation. Probably, having selected your method, you are reasoning backwards to the problem of teenage smoking and the need to prevent it.

Another example: you may tackle the broad problem of infant mortality. You could concentrate on low birth weight and prematurity, teenage mothers, and prenatal care. But you are a neonatal intensive care unit (NICU); you want to address the high-risk infants who are discharged from NICUs; so you deal with parental behavior.

Whether or not you expect to show changes in the broad problem during the life of the project, you will definitely have to present data to document the specific contributing problems manifested in your target population. Present baseline data, and if possible or relevant, contrast these with national or other similar data to show the local magnitude of the problem. These baseline data are the basis for proving change by the end of the project. Institutional data are a rich source.

The comments in the section above on the broad problem and the value of presenting needs assessment data also apply here, unless the entire project is designed as a needs assessment study. As an example, the graduate writing skills project could develop a questionnaire asking program directors or graduate advisors how many matriculated and nonmatriculated students are in their programs, how many applicants are rejected for reasons of writing in an average year, how many matriculated students are lost due to writing deficiencies in a year, how many are borderline, and how many could benefit from an intermediate-level graduate course in writing. You could ask for some of the data by sex and ethnicity, and the number for whom English is a second language.

WRITING ABOUT THE CONTRIBUTING PROBLEMS

In writing about the contributing problems you draw on the literature of the field. You show the reader that you are aware of the complexity of the broad problem by acknowledging the many contributing problems. Then you explain why you chose the particular one or two you are addressing. Show the significance of these particular contributing problems, and refer to the literature in the field to support your focus on the particular one(s) with which you will deal. Show how the aspects you will tackle are central to the problem and that your agency is capable of handling these within the project period.

The contributing problems you select are the ones you are promising to show reductions in by the end of the project. Even though you haven't written a word about objectives yet, you are really introducing these particular problems because you hope to affect them. The others are included in your statement to show your grasp of the field.

You would include the data from your needs assessment by making the major points in the text and presenting a table showing the actual data. You might include the original questionnaire as an appendix. Whether or not you do a needs assessment, you would present baseline data and, if possible or relevant, contrast these with national or other similar data to show the local magnitude of the problem. These baseline data become the basis for proving change by the end of the project. Institutional data are a rich source to support your case.

INTERMEDIARY PROBLEMS

In health, education, social services, and similar fields, contributing problems often include the behavior of individuals, institutions, or governments. These behaviors, if changed, could help ameliorate the broad problem. In these people-oriented fields there is a major commitment to the concept that the way to effect behavioral change is to change beliefs, attitudes, or knowledge. There is a commitment to educational solutions. Not everyone expects education alone to do the job; but this is a common method in these fields. Please note that *an educational solution requires a statement about an educational problem.*

Programs to educate or change attitudes are not really undertaken just for themselves; rather, they are undertaken in the hope that they will change behavior. For this reason, because the problems of belief and knowledge are indirect (they are relevant only because of a given theory of cause and effect), they can be called *intermediary problems.* An intermediary problem is really a causal factor underlying a contributing problem; it is a contributing problem one step removed from the broad problem. This distinction is important, because it represents a chain of effects based on a theoretical structure. One educates in order to change behavior that, in turn, is expected to affect the broad problem.

The fields that focus on educational methods to bring about change are particularly deficient in literature that demonstrates the linkage between educational effectiveness, behavioral change, and changes in broad problems. Skipping the link between education and behavior means ignoring information about causality and the behavior. Partly this is because it is difficult to collect information that measures behavior. It is easier to collect data on broad problem status and educational test results.

Since the broad problem is generally multicausal, and the link between education and behavior is rarely documented, evaluation of the effectiveness of education as a method is impossible, or spurious conclusions are drawn, or educational solutions continue to be supported in the absence of real proof that they work.

If your project is designed to tackle your target group's lack of information or knowledge, or negative attitudes, or institutional conditions that support negative behavior, you are dealing with intermediary problems. It is important that you make clear the underlying hypothesis abut the effect of the intermediary problem on the behavioral problem, because you will later have to justify your selection of an educational method to solve a behavioral problem.

In the project oriented to the problem of infant mortality and morbidity among NICU graduates, the behavioral problems have to do with lack of follow-up clinic care and the lack of parental care-giving and monitoring for signs of developmental disabilities. The educational problems are (1) not knowing the importance of the follow-up care, (2) not knowing how to provide the parenting, and (3) not knowing what is needed and what to monitor. In the project dealing with heart-attack victims, the behavioral problem is the need to supply the new medication as soon as possible. The intermediary problem is that paramedics don't know how to administer the medication in the field.

Not all projects will have all three problem levels. Research projects may not have intermediary problems; but an analogue may be that, to test a certain hypothesis, normative data must first be collected. The lack of normative data may be treated as an intermediary problem.

WRITING ABOUT THE INTERMEDIARY PROBLEMS

If you have provided a listing for yourself of the broad and contributing problems, you should be able to look at each behavioral problem to determine whether there is an educational or institutional problem that, if solved, would make the behaviors change (based on the hypothesis or belief you subscribe to).

It makes sense to present the intermediary problems in parallel with the behavioral problems and refer to the interactions. Here again, the literature of the field, supporting the link between the educational problems and the behaviors, should be drawn on in the narrative. If you present intermediary problems, provide baseline data for your target population if you can. You may refer to the literature to give reasonable estimates of the local problem. Needs assessment or institutional data are especially valuable, and the comments presented earlier apply.

SIGNIFICANCE OF THE PROBLEMS

In writing the problem statement, you establish the significance of your problems by showing national relevance, the severity for the target population, and the benefits if solved. The strongest evidence of significance you can provide for a community-based program is a needs assessment that has been conducted among the target population, giving the unique situation for your project focus or showing that these proposed clients consider the problem significant. (Later, it will be important to show that the clients are enthusiastic about the method.) If the people involved consider the problem important or were involved in identifying the problem, the project can be expected to have a greater likelihood of success; that is important to the funding agency. In arguing the significance of the problem, make a compelling case, but do not lecture the reader.

For specific disease and research problems, the comparable indication of significance should come from experts, professionals, and the literature, showing that your subject selection is appropriate or that you are dealing with the next area of research in a sequence being addressed by the professional community.

PRACTICAL TIPS

1. *Remember that the problem is never that your program does not exist.* Your problem is not, for example, that parents are not being trained in parenting, or that there are no programs involving inner-city youth with the art community. That "begs the question," or stacks the argument, because you are naming *your* program method. The problem is what the method is trying to help, such as parents not knowing how to provide follow-up care, or inner-city youth not opting for arts careers and not being audiences for the arts.

2. There should be a problem statement for every objective that you propose to deliver. Before writing the final proposal, using the outline presented later in this book, be sure that every program objective relates back to a problem statement.

3. The following outline may be useful:

Broad problem. The main reason for the project. Give background, significance. Document with data. Localize to your target population. Document with data.

Contributing problem(s) (behavioral problems). Show the theoretical connections with causes of the broad problem. Identify those the project will address and justify. Provide baseline data, especially for the target population. Show significance.

Intermediary problems (educational problems). If applicable. Show the theoretical connections to the contributing problems. Provide baseline data. Show significance.

This outline is then followed in parallel by the objectives and methods sections. Exhibit 10, in Chapter 9, shows the way the sections interconnect. Before writing these three sections it is best to read

Chapters 6 through 9. It is not wise to start writing without working on a schematic outline, which will help you clarify the project ideas and shorten the final writing time.

4. Examples of problem/needs statements appear in Exhibit 7. In the first example the statement is quite long, reflecting the detail that would be required for a federal proposal. The second is shorter, and is more appropriate for a concept paper or a foundation application. The superscripts in the texts are hypothetical footnote references citing sources for the statements made, but not given here or in other examples.

EXHIBIT 7
Examples of Problem/Needs Statements

Example 1: Education for Parents of Infants Discharged from Intensive Care

THE PROBLEM

Broad Problem

The decline in infant mortality rates has slowed in the 1980s. And despite the long-term decline in infant mortality in the United States there are major disparities by area, reflecting the disproportionate rates for Blacks and children born to parents in poverty. In 1985 the infant mortality rate was 10.6 per 1,000 live births; the rate for Whites was 9.3, and the rate for Blacks was 18.2. In central-city communities such as____, served by ____ Hospital Center, the rate was 12.5, with some communities experiencing rates as high as 23.3.[1] By 1986 the available data show an overall decline in infant mortality rates, to 10.4, but the rates for communities such as ____ and ____ had climbed to 27.6 and 19.1, even while the rate for the city as a whole declined.

Mortality rates are traditionally subdivided for reporting into three time intervals: *perinatal mortality,* covering the birth period, *neonatal mortality,* covering infants from birth to 27 days, and *postneonatal mortality,* covering infants 28 days to 11 months. The White/Black disparity is reflected in the subdivision rates. In 1985 the White perinatal rate was 9.6, and the Black, 17.4. The neonatal rate was 6.1 for Whites and 12.1 for Blacks, while the postneonatal rate was 3.2 for Whites and 6.1 for Blacks.

Clearly, the largest problem is reflected in the perinatal and neonatal periods. In these areas the focus has been on preventing low birth weight, which is the single most important predictor for infant mortality. Programs to provide prenatal care and prevent risk behaviors in mothers have been focused on prevention.

Neonatal mortality is considered to have been most influenced by endogenous or medical causes, such as the development of neonatal intensive care units (NICUs) and their high-technology interventions. On the other hand, postneonatal mortality has been thought to reflect environmental or social causes of death.[2]

The 1990 Federal Priority Objectives for Pregnancy and Infant Health had no goal for postneonatal mortality. Yet many of the factors affecting low birth weight are the

continued

same factors that place the neonatal survivor at risk of death before the first year of life. The educational levels of the parents and their financial status, both indexes of poverty and race, correlate with birth weight and infant mortality, as do malnutrition, severe chronic stress, and the mother's being under 18. The birth-weight distribution has changed little in the past 25 years. And in 1986 the rate of postneonatal mortality actually rose, from 3.6 in 1985 to 3.7 in 1986.[3]

The neonatal survivors who are at risk are, in large part, the neonatal survivors of low birth weight. Premature infants are about 10 percent of live births, of which 90 percent who are two to three pounds at birth survive. About 70 percent of those born weighing less than two pounds survive, largely due to care received in the nation's 420 neonatal intensive care units.

NICU care for a severely underweight infant can last over three months until discharge. A typical NICU has room for 18 infants; the ____ Center can care for 30, with approximately 20 discharged each month. There are also intermediate-care facilities. In addition, infants with severe handicaps may survive but cannot be sent to their homes. It is the 20 infants per month, coming from homes in the inner city and of young mothers, Blacks or Hispanics or immigrants, and/or with poverty backgrounds, that we are addressing. At the ____ Center, for infants about whom we can find data 11 months after birth, we have figures that are triple the national postneonatal mortality rate.[4]

The low birth-weight neonatal survivors are at risk for developmental delays, illness, and death once they leave the NICUs. A sizable percentage of infants of very low birth weight face severe handicaps that require prolonged treatment and alertness for sudden respiratory and cardiac distress. A study carried out by Jane Hunt at the University of California[5] found that the long-term predictors of longevity for premature infants are how sick the babies were and the educational level of the family; the latter is an index of poverty and the home environment.

Contributing Problems

Given low birth weight and prematurity, there has not been sufficient attention to providing adequate follow-up care for infants who leave intensive care. Efforts to reduce postneonatal deaths for infants with birth weights of less than five pounds must address access to and utilization of medical care, and the sources of such care must include those closest to the infants, the mothers and other caretakers at home.

Among the problems contributing to the morbidity and mortality of infants after discharge from NICUs is that the care-giving behaviors are not being performed once the infants are home. Many experts believe that the parents need help that extends beyond the NICU, including clinic follow-up.[6]

A raft of behaviors is neglected in poverty homes headed by one or more young parents, who generally have little educational background and no training in parental skills.

1. A prime problem is the need for follow-up care for the infants because of the danger of illness and developmental difficulties. The parents tend not to seek the proper follow-up medical care for their infants.

continued

2. These parents often lack proper parenting behavior to fill the needs of the infants, such as proper stimulation, nurturing behavior, nutritional needs, exercise, and infection control practices.

3. The parents generally lack behaviors that can save the lives of their children in medical emergencies, such as cardiopulmonary resuscitation (CPR) and antichoking maneuvers.

4. The parents are not providing the monitoring skills to spot developmental delays and other complications and are therefore not seeking medical help for such symptoms as delays in crawling, walking, and talking and slow weight gain.

Preliminary interviews with 20 mothers of NICU patients at the ____ Hospital Center indicate that almost all felt deficient in ability to perform most of the activities mentioned above, and all felt deficient in at least three.[7]

Educational Problems

The contributing problems describe the behaviors lacking in infant caregivers and are related to what parents do not know and did not learn about the health and risk status of their infants, and the parents' lack of the knowledge and skills needed to improve the outcomes for their special infants. The parents do not provide the activities needed by the infants because they lack information and do not understand the difference they can make. Among the knowledge lacks are the following:

1. What follow-up care for the infants is available, how it can be obtained, why the infant is at risk and needs the follow-up, and the conditions under which coming to a clinic is desirable.

2. How or when or why to provide care such as stimulation, nurturing behavior, nutrition, exercise, and infection control practices, and how these apply to their homes.

3. How and when to apply medical emergency care such as cardiopulmonary resuscitation (CPR) and antichoking maneuvers.

4. The need for and how to spot developmental delays and other complications, and when to seek medical help for such symptoms as delays in crawling, walking, and talking and slow weight gain.

Target Population

The project proposes to address the problems described at ____ Hospital Center. It will serve 300 to 500 parents of the 300 infants expected to be discharged during the months the program will be in operation, assuming a targeted start-up date by the end of the seventh project month and a three-year funding period. The parents and their 300 infants represent a cross-section of the city, but are heavily represented by inner-city and minority populations. From 40 to 60 percent of the infants are transferred from other community hospitals without NICU facilities. The majority are Black or Hispanic, with middle to low income levels. Most of the mothers are 16 to 35 years of

continued

age; half are single parents. While most have completed high school, about 20 percent have not. Most are inexperienced, first-time parents.

Eligible parents will be those with infants being treated at the hospital's NICU. The infants will be ready for discharge planning and identified as at high or moderate risk for recurring illness, physical disabilities, or developmental delays. The "parents" eligible will include the natural mother and/or any one or two immediate caregivers in the home, including support persons close to single parents.

Example 2: Ambulance Staff Training in Emergency Medical Services

PROBLEM

Main Problem

According to the American Heart Association, in 1987 approximately 1 million people in the United States were expected to suffer acute myocardial infarctions — heart attacks. Approximately one-half were expected to die.[1] *The majority of the deaths occur before the victim reaches a hospital.* Survivors of heart attacks show varying degrees of disability, depending on the extent of the damage to the heart muscle, and this often relates directly to *how quickly patients receive therapeutic intervention.*

Contributing Problems

There is an accepted method of reducing mortality and morbidity among heart attack victims: the intravenous infusion of streptokinase, a clot-dissolving medication. The streptokinase must be administered quickly, while the infarct, or damage to the heart muscle, is still underway. The earlier it is administered, the more beneficial it is to the patient outcome.[2]

Studies agree that patient outcome is improved when streptokinase is administered during the first two to three hours after the onset of symptoms (classically, crushing substernal chest pain), and that the very highest success at salvaging the heart muscle, and thus the most significant decrease in morbidity and mortality, occurs when streptokinase is administered within an hour after the onset of the symptoms.[3]

The chief contributing problem addressed by this project is the difficulty in getting streptokinase to patients suffering heart attacks more quickly. Currently, at the ____ Hospital, streptokinase is administered in the emergency department to patients presenting with an acute myocardial infarction. The hospital staff has demonstrated that patients suffering from a heart attack who arrive in the emergency room via ambulance receive streptokinase therapy, on average, almost 90 minutes after the onset of their chest pain.[4]

A second contributing problem is the need to be sure that the drug is administered safely. Streptokinase is not a risk-free medication. It has always been administered with a physician present. Patients who receive streptokinase can sometimes suffer a severe allergic reaction, but the most serious side effect is bleeding. The most significant contraindication to the administration of streptokinase is the presence of a bleeding disorder. A patient who is to be infused with streptokinase must not have a history of bleeding peptic ulcer, recent CVA (stroke), recent streptococcal infection,

continued

severe hypertension, recent major surgery, or recent serious trauma. The patient also must not be pregnant.

The problem, then, is how to provide streptokinase safely in the field prior to arrival at the hospital. Paramedics would be in communication with and under the medical control of a base station physician, as always, but there would now be the need to correctly select patients and then safely administer the drug.

A review of the vital statistics for _____ City, covering the past 5 years, indicates that at least 1,000 residents of the catchment area served by the _____ Hospital's ambulance service will suffer a heart attack in a given year. The _____ Hospital's paramedics currently treat and transport 150 of these patients annually. A preliminary review indicates that at least 50 of these patients would meet the criteria for receiving streptokinase therapy in the field. The patients reflect the age distribution for this type of disease and are 50 percent Black and Hispanic.

Intermediary Problems

The critical intermediary problem is educational. The 17 full-time and 20 per-diem paramedics who make up the hospital's ambulance team are not able to administer streptokinase in the field prior to transport because they have never been trained to do so.

The first need would be to gain agreement on the part of the paramedics and their collective bargaining representatives to receive the training.

Although they currently monitor the heart rate and rhythm of cardiac patients, paramedics do not know how to perform a diagnostic 12-lead EKG and transmit the results to a base-station physician to confirm the presence of an acute myocardial infarction.

Paramedics do not know the indications, contraindications, and possible side effects of administering the drug, or the procedure to follow to obtain the necessary information in the field, or how to respond to side effects.

Paramedics do not know the procedure to administer streptokinase. Additionally, the 12 base-station physicians, medical attending physicians in the emergency department, are currently not trained in the appropriate procedural guidelines to follow to provide medical control for paramedics who are to administer streptokinase in the field.

7

Basic Components of the Proposal: Objectives

INTRODUCTION

The objectives of a project are its expected accomplishments. These are promises you make to the funding agency. As with all promises, you get into the least trouble by being clear about what you are promising, about when you are promising to deliver, and about how you expect to show that you have delivered what you promised. You do this by making specific, usually quantifiable statements about changes in the problem situations you are addressing, by attaching due dates, and by giving some idea of how the results will be measured. The measurement of the results prefigures the evaluation design, which will be discussed later in this book.

This section divides the statements of objectives into several parts, to clarify what is involved with the various types of end results that a project can deliver. It closely parallels the outline of the problem/needs statement.

LONG-RANGE GOALS

Long-range goals are desired changes in the *broad problem*. These will eventually be brought about, but not until after the project period is ended. This terminology separates goals from objectives by noting whether results can be observed by the end of the project period. A broad problem has been defined as one with a complex causality, the amelioration of which is the ultimate aim of the project. If you do not expect to see changes within the project time frame, you have a *goal*. Recall the example of the smoking-cessation program. A reduction in the rate of lung cancer would not be expected to show up within a one- or two-year period. Similarly, a project to introduce inner-city youth to the arts community would not show effects in terms of audience attendance or entry into arts careers after only one year.

Objectives, however, are achievable within the project period. If you expect to measure changes in the broad problem, you have an objective, not a goal.

WRITING THE STATEMENT OF GOALS

To help in the logical flow of the proposal, the section on objectives is written in parallel with the section on problem/needs. You would begin with the long-range goals, reflecting the broad problem. If you expect to show changes in the broad problem, you will not need a section on long-range goals. In the case of the parent-education project, the long-range goal would be accelerated decline in infant mortality and parity between Black and White postneonatal mortality rates. Since this project *will* be able to demonstrate reductions in the postneonatal mortality and morbidity rates for the *target population,* there will be both a long-range goal and a project objective to match the broad problem/needs section.

When writing a goals section, indicate why expectation of reaching the goals is outside the project's time frame, and how the project is expected to move toward their attainment. The goals are stated in terms of the decline of the broad problem in the target population.

PROJECT OBJECTIVES

Project objectives are the expected changes and end results you say the project will accomplish within the funding period. Project objectives can be changes in health status or behaviors or institutional functioning; they can also be the presence of something that was not there before, such as a facility. In research the objective can be the proof of a hypothesis or of the validity of data, or some other quantitative end result promised. *Project objectives,* compared with *process objectives,* are end results that affect the problems directly. Process objectives are things that must be produced or accomplished to make the project objectives possible, and stem from the methods used.

You will want to target changes that you can reasonably expect to achieve. Sometimes the literature of the field gives you targets you can expect to meet or exceed. For new methods or populations, you have to make educated guesses about what you can deliver: enough to make the funding worthwhile, but not so much that you set yourself up to fail.

We can call project objectives broad objectives, main objectives, behavioral objectives, administrative objectives, educational objectives, or intermediary objectives — depending on what problem statements they match. You are expected to have one or more project objectives for each problem you introduce; they are the end results of the project, as seen from the funder's point of view. This section describes project objectives in a manner similar to the way problem statements were described in Chapter 6.

Broad Objectives, Main Objectives

If you expect to be able to measure declines in the broad problem among your target population or in your target institution, these expected changes are project objectives. You would specify the changes you expect to show by giving the expected magnitude of the change and the expected due date, usually by the end of the project period. If you presented baseline data for your problem statement, you would predict changes in the same type of measure for your target population.

Behavioral Objectives

Behavioral objectives are behavioral changes in the contributing problems that you expect to show by the end of the project period. You may have several of these to match your detailed listing of the contributing problems. If your contributing problems are not behavioral, as in a research project, you may not wish to give these objectives a separate name. They would still be project objectives.

Assuming you included baseline data when you presented your problems, you would incorporate the expected changes in those data as part of your statement of objectives. You would usually need to indicate some quantitative change in the contributing problems as manifested in the target population or situation.

For example, you may want to show that streptokinase is being administered safely in the field, or that parental behavior is being demonstrated as desired, or that students are achieving the writing goals set at the beginning of the project, or that women of color are achieving leadership positions in antiviolence agencies or are speaking up at conferences.

In some of these cases you may be hard-pressed to come up with a way to demonstrate a quantitative change in behavior. You might use records to count clinic visits, and charts to assess side effects of medication; you might use attendance records in classes or grades; but how would you measure parental behavior? or changes in sexual behavior? or changes in violent behavior? or changes in career goals?

You are called on to be creative in your measures of behavioral change. You may consider simulation situations to project probable behavior; traditionally, self-reporting has been used, with allowances for the likelihood of incorrect recall or desire to please the interviewer. You may be able to come up with new, useful measures. A good source is the literature in the field, reporting on prior project activities in your subject area.

The problems of measuring the success of the objectives are actually faced in the evaluation design, and under process objectives if you will be creating test instruments. All that you need for your statement of project objectives is the extent of the predicted changes.

Intermediary Objectives

If you had intermediary/educational problems, you will have intermediary/educational objectives. Educational objectives are not hard to state, since knowledge can be measured in traditional ways, with tests. You really need only take the problem statement and convert it into a statement of improvement. The challenge is to make sure that the tests are at an appropriate reading/writing level for the target population, that they reflect the content you wish mastered, and that they distinguish between competent and novice levels of knowledge.

The parent education project will be demonstrating that the parents learned the material taught; the streptokinase project will test the paramedics' new knowledge; and the writing project will be looking at writing grades.

PROCESS OBJECTIVES

Process objectives have to do with the functioning of the project. These are activities you promise to carry out or products you promise to create in order to carry out the project. They do not correspond directly to problem statements. Process objectives relate to specific project objectives and are generated by your methodology. You promise them because you need them in order to deliver the method; they enable. Because of their role in making the work of the project possible, they are usually due early in the project.

One kind of process objective is a *product*. You may have to design and test a data-collection instrument, or design a curriculum, or produce the instruction on tape. These are all products, because you need to be funded to produce them. Note that if you merely need funding to purchase test instruments or equipment or instructional tapes, you would have a budget item, not a product. For it to be a product objective, your project must promise to create it.

Another kind of process objective is a *milestone*. You may promise to reach a specific number in your outreach activities or have enrollment targets; you may promise a promotional event; you may promise to obtain approval of plans from a board or administrator; you may promise to have your staff trained to participate in a new service function. These are accomplishments needed for the project to function, and are milestone objectives. Figure 7.1 shows the relationships of the various categories of objectives.

FIGURE 7.1
Kinds of Objectives

1. LONG RANGE GOALS (BEYOND PROJECT TIME FRAME)	
2. PROJECT OBJECTIVES	3. PROCESS OBJECTIVES
BROAD / MAIN	
BEHAVIORAL / ADMINISTRATIVE	PRODUCTS
INTERMEDIARY / EDUCATIONAL	MILESTONES

WRITING THE STATEMENT OF OBJECTIVES

The statement of objectives should run parallel with the problem/needs statement, and, though not every project will have all types of objectives, every problem presented earlier should have at least one corresponding project objective. It is a good idea to tell the reader to what problem an objective refers.

Process objectives can be called "related process objectives" and can be listed after each group of objectives to which they relate. You can also list the project objectives and then present the process objectives in chronological order of their due dates. Your decision should be based on the manner of presentation that is clearest to the reader.

Each objective should be stated in measurable terms so that it can later be evaluated in terms of your success in meeting the quality, quantity, and/or due dates you set for it. You therefore will be predicting the magnitude of the change as well as the direction of the change. For sample populations you may also be talking about statistically significant change.

Each objective should begin or end with a due date. You can group objectives under common due dates. You need not name a calendar date; it might be "by the end of the sixth month" or "by the end of the project period." The objective would then include the achievement met, by whom, followed by a phrase beginning, "as measured by," followed by some indication of the measuring instrument.

Process objectives are usually stated in measurable terms, but the measures tend to be due dates, an indication of administrative or professional approval, and/or target numbers. These are incorporated into the statement of the objective.

PRACTICAL TIPS

1. In your first writing of the objectives, it is enough to just indicate the direction of change and some idea of the criterion; during the initial stages of project planning, the evaluation design is not a major focus. But it may be useful to glance at the chapters on evaluation design. When you have designed the evaluation section of the project, you can refine your objectives. In the first example presented in Exhibit 8, the statement of objectives reflects prior work on the evaluation design. The second example represents an earlier stage in the writing process.

2. A set of project and process objectives can be introduced by a descriptive paragraph and then take the form of a numbered set of short paragraphs; it need not take up much space.

3. Remember, since the problem cannot be the lack of your project, *delivering the program cannot be a project objective.* However, getting the program on-stream by a specific date may be a process objective (a milestone).

4. The following outline may be useful.

Long-range goals. Changes in the broad problem beyond the period of the project.

Project objectives
Broad objectives, and/or behavioral objectives. Promised outcomes or changes in broad or contributing problems. Give due dates, quality and quantity changes, and the way they are to be measured. Follow the order of the problem statements.

Educational/intermediary objectives. Promised changes in the intermediary problems. Give their due dates, quality and quantity changes, and the way they are to be measured. Follow the order of the problem statements.

Related Process Objectives. Products or milestones needed to carry out the project methods. Give the due dates, quality and quantity criteria, and the way they are to be measured. Follow the chronological order of their due dates.

5. Remember that the process objectives are generated by your methods. The actual writing is done by working from the problems to the objectives, to the methods, and back to the process objectives.

Before writing the objectives, it is best to read Chapters 6, 7, 8, and 9 and develop an outline for your project based on Exhibit 10, in Chapter 9.

EXHIBIT 8
Examples of Statement of Objectives

Example 1: Education for Parents of Infants Discharged from Intensive Care

OBJECTIVES

Long-Range Goals

The main problems addressed by the project are the deceleration in the decline of postneonatal mortality and the continued disparity between the Black and other minority members' rate and the White rate. The long-range goal of the program is accelerated decline in neonatal mortality and parity between Whites and other groups. These goals are not attainable within the three-year period for the proposed project.

However, by demonstrating that education of parents for post-NICU care of their infants and postdischarge follow-up care can reduce the risks, the project may lead the way in reducing those cases of postneonatal mortality and morbidity that are attributable to inadequate home conditions, lack of access to care, and insufficiency of parenting knowledge.

Project Objectives/Main Objectives

It is within the scope of the project objectives to demonstrate declines in mortality, illness, and developmental delays within the target population.

1. By the end of the project period, for infants discharged from the NICU at ____ Hospital whose caregivers have received pre- and post-discharge training in infant care and the need to pursue follow-up clinic care, 18 months after discharge the mortality rates will be 20 percent lower than the mortality rates for comparable

continued

infants 18 months after discharge in the period preceding the start of the educational program, as measured by hospital and follow-up health and death records.

2. By the end of the project period, for infants discharged from the NICU at ____ Hospital whose caregivers received pre- and post-discharge training in infant care and the need to pursue follow-up clinic care, 18 months after discharge the morbidity and delayed developmental problem rates will be 25 percent lower than the same rates for comparable infants 18 months after discharge in the period preceding the start of the educational program, as measured by hospital and follow-up health records.

Project Objectives/Behavioral Objectives

The main objectives are expected to be the result of behavioral changes on the part of the parents who receive the training.

3. By the end of the 30th month of the project, 90 percent of the infants whose caregivers received pre- and post-discharge training in infant care and the need to pursue follow-up clinic care will be complying with recommended schedules of visits to the follow-up clinic, as measured by clinic records.

4. By the end of the 30th month, the participating caregivers will demonstrate appropriate parenting behavior, proper response to emergencies, and appropriate monitoring of developmental delays as measured by scores of 85 percent or better on simulation tests of the required behavior and major increases in post-test scores among those with low pre-test scores.

Project Objectives/Educational Objectives

The behavioral objectives are expected to be met through the educational program, which is the heart of the project design.

5. Upon completion of the training, the caregivers will produce scores of 85 percent or better on paper-and-pencil knowledge tests covering the knowledge necessary for the behavioral objectives to be attained. They will show major increases in post-test scores among those with low pre-test scores.

Process Objectives

The following objectives represent targeted products to be produced and milestones to be reached to enable the project objectives to be reached.

By the end of the first month:

6. The curriculum content for the educational program will be approved by the senior staff and faculty at ____ College.

By the end of the seventh month:

7. The video tapes for the program will be ready for use in three languages and approved by a review committee that includes representatives of the target parent population.

continued

8. Staff members will be trained to lead the discussion groups and will have been successfully evaluated by the senior staff.
9. Outreach material describing the training and clinic services will be ready for use.
10. Procedures for referral to training and clinic services will be in place.
11. Clinic services will be available.
12. The training program will be on-stream.
13. Record forms for use in data collection and evaluation will be in place.
14. Pre- and post-tests of behavior, using video simulation, and paper-and-pencil knowledge tests will be field tested and ready for use.

By the end of the 36th month:

15. Of those infants eligible for their caregivers' participation in the program, 95 percent will have one or more caregivers actively involved; 80 percent of caregivers will successfully complete the training.
16. Tapes and program materials will be available to interested NICUs and others. Evaluation results will be available for distribution.

Example 3: City Children Involved in the Arts Community

LONG-RANGE GOALS

The project's long-range goals are outside the scope of the one-year pilot project, but it is hoped that if the project is successful, it will move the city closer to attainment of the following:

1. An increase in the audience for the arts among inner-city residents.
2. An increase in the number of inner-city youth who opt for careers in the arts.
3. For all inner-city youth, an experience of what it is like to be in the art world and what it is like to work as an artist.

Project Objectives

As a result of the project's existence, the following will be accomplished by the end of the project year:

1. One thousand of the students attending inner-city elementary and junior high schools will have had the experience of what it is like to live and work in the art community of ____.
2. The students will each have the experience of being in an audience or attending a gallery show in the arts.
3. A minimum of five projects expressing issues of the inner city will be begun by participating artists and will involve, on average, five students per project after the pilot project year is over.
4. Twenty-five students or more will sign up for this further work with participating artists.
5. Teachers at the students' schools will be involved with the participating artists in integrating the experiences into the classrooms.

continued

6. The students will be able to articulate what kinds of art careers and art audience experiences are open to them.

Process Objectives

To make these objectives possible, the following will be done in the first months of the project:

1. Review committees and artist/teacher committees will be established before the students start attending sessions.
2. Student and separate teacher evaluation forms will be designed.
3. A master plan selecting the schools, scheduling the sessions, and identifying the students will be prepared before the first sessions begin.
4. A means of allowing the students to select an art form for their sessions will be designed, and 80 percent of the students will receive assignments reflecting their preferences.

8

Basic Components of the Proposal: Methods

PROJECT ACTIVITY AS METHOD

When you commit yourself to project objectives, you commit to carrying out activities to bring them about. These activities are the methods you will use to reach the objectives. The methods for reaching the project objectives are generally the central activities of the project, and the description of your methods is the heart of your proposal. This is what you are asking to be funded to do. You should provide the most information and detail in this section.

Every objective you write about, including every process objective, must be matched with a method statement. While you may have more than one method of reaching an objective, or one method to reach several objectives, the reader should be able to find each objective's corresponding method statement. This is done by following a logical sequence parallel to the statement of objectives or a chronological sequence, referring the reader to the objectives being discussed.

Methods for the Long-Range Goals

If you have long-range goals, you will not have a project method for them, as such. But it is appropriate to indicate in a theoretical statement how the project's main methodology is expected to bring the broad problems nearer solution.

Methods for the Main Project Objectives and/or Behavioral Objectives

The methods of reaching the main project objectives, which may be behavioral objectives, are the central focus of the methods section. You should make it clear exactly what is going to be delivered: the content, form, sequencing, numbers to be served, and target population characteristics; and the number of cycles of the basic program that will be covered in the project period. Comments on the staff members and their qualifications are also appropriate. (In a research project, the method is your research design.)

Methods for Intermediary/Educational Objectives

If you have intermediary objectives, especially if they are educational objectives, the education or intermediary service you will provide is the method corresponding to the behavioral objectives. The method for an intermediary/educational objective is the way the educational or other intermediary service will be delivered. For example, in the case of the parent education program, there will be lessons on VCR, discussion groups, and tapes available in three languages. You provide details about how you will deliver the educational program.

Methods for the Process Objectives

Each process objective also requires a method statement. You are expected to describe just how you will reach your outreach target, how you will design the curriculum, or get board approval, or design the interview protocol. The process objectives are generated by the main project methods, so remember to go back and develop methods for the process objectives once they are formulated.

JUSTIFICATION OF PROJECT METHODS

When presenting project methods you make an implicit hypothesis that by using a given method you will accomplish a given objective. The funding agency must be convinced that you have chosen the best, most appropriate method for the task. Justify your choice. You can draw on the literature of the field. Refer to the alternative methods and show how the one you have selected is the best for your specific situation. You may wish to discuss what has been successful or what has failed elsewhere.

You may show why your method deals with issues that have never been addressed before. Your subject matter will determine what you draw on, but you must demonstrate that you know the relevant options as presented in the literature and that you have selected those most practical and useful.

At the broadest level, the method may be only a statement that an educational approach or an administrative approach is appropriate. But remember that there are alternatives even at this level. *Why* education? *Why* that particular administrative approach?

WRITING AND SEQUENCING THE METHODS SECTION

After presenting the theoretical statement that provides the reader with a broad, logical description of the main project methods, you may wish to give your justification for these main methods. The justification can also be incorporated into the descriptions of the separate project methods.

You cover the project objectives one by one, grouping those with a common method and justification. You may prefer to make a statement about the method of reaching the long-range goal and then present the objectives in order of their due dates, or you may go from the process objectives, to intermediary objectives, to the behavioral objectives. That way each step will build on the logic of the prior step.

You may wish to introduce each section by a sentence presenting the relevant objective(s), as follows: To bring about (state objective), the following will be done. That sets the context. Then you justify the selection of the method.

It is appropriate to group those of your objectives that can be dealt with by a common method. For example, if you have educational problems and educational objectives, a particular kind of training program with a certain kind of teaching format may be appropriate for each educational objective. Remember that the methodology of educational programs includes the content (what you will teach), which is the method for your behavioral objectives, and the techniques of instruction (how you will teach), which is the method for your educational objectives.

These last distinctions are not crucial. If you combine your methods sections on behavioral and educational objectives it is not the end of the world, but it is important to cover all the information that such a detailed outline elicits.

PRACTICAL TIPS

1. Remember to include the numbers: the frequency of a service, the length of an educational component; the number of separate presentations of a program cycle within a project year, and the total to be served during the entire project period.

2. Remember to describe staffing.

3. It is helpful to place each objective on an index card, with its method. Then create a card for each step of the method. Arrange the cards in time sequence. See that each milestone and product is also represented, with the steps for these. Then check your time sequence again to see what the actual time period for the project must be. You may want to revise your concept or scope.

4. You may confuse process objectives with methods. The difference is that process objectives refer to a time at which something will be achieved, an end point. Method refers to a process over time that gets you to that end point.

5. Help the reader follow your reasoning and sequencing.

6. Be sure that you are able to deliver the activities you are promising.

7. Be sure your agency will support each step.

8. Read your statement of method. Is each objective represented by a method? Does the narrative provide a picture of what you will be doing in chronological order? Is the thinking clear? Can you get a picture of the way the project will be carried out?

9. Exhibit 9 presents examples of the methods section.

10. Before writing the methods section, develop the outline based on Exhibit 10 in Chapter 9.

EXHIBIT 9
Examples of Methods Statements

Example 1: Education for Parents of Infants Discharged from Intensive Care

METHODS

The primary method proposed in the project design is geared to reduce the morbidity and mortality among graduates of neonatal intensive care units (NICUs). It is focused on the unmet needs of poverty and minority families, supplying the

continued

education and clinical follow-up needed to reduce postneonatal mortality, morbidity, and developmental disorders. The method becomes one more vital link in the chain of steps to reduce infant mortality nationally and to reduce disparities among population groups.

The methodology, aside from the provision of clinic follow-up care, is educational, addressed to mothers and other caregivers before discharge. It has been shown that responsive caregiving and supportive environments can be instrumental in preventing illness and early developmental deficits.[8] In Chicago $1 million is being spent to establish a multiservice center for successful child development. A major focus is on providing parents of NICU graduates with help in rearing children.[9]

The ____ Hospital center has been successful in patient education programs in areas of family planning and prenatal care because from their initial design the programs have included representatives of the target population. The method can be carried out with minor expenditure of funds and is cost-efficient, justifying the high costs of NICU care as longevity expectations are increased.

The clinic-based follow-up program for high risk infants will be patterned on the one in use at the Children's Hospital of ____,[10] adapted to meet the needs of the target population at ____ Hospital. Permission to use the curriculum has been obtained from ____. See Appendix __.

Methods for Project Objectives

The project will accommodate the eligible infants and caregivers of the approximately 20 infants who are discharged from the ____ NICU monthly, from the 8th to the 36th project month, or approximately 300+ infants, of whom about 120 will be followed for evaluation purposes for 18 months. It is expected that half the infants will have one caregiver represented and one half will have two involved in the program, so about 500 caregivers are expected to participate.

To be eligible the infant must be at risk for recurring illness or developmental delays; or have a handicapping condition such as chronic lung disease, brain damage; or have congenital anomalies; or have had a birth weight of 2,000 grams or less, requiring a prolonged or difficult hospitalization. Individual factors include severity of initial illness, length of time in NICU, and weight at birth. Additional factors will include the economic status of the mother and the home situation. Infants at lesser risk will be eligible in months when fewer than 20 infants meet the higher eligibility criteria.

The eligible caregivers are those adults immediately responsible for the care of the infant upon discharge, such as the natural mother and father, the foster parents, or adults living with the mother who will be involved in the caregiving.

To reach the objectives of 90 percent follow-up clinic care and 85 percent of caregivers demonstrating appropriate parenting behavior, proper response to emergencies and appropriate monitoring of developmental delays, the following will be done:

continued

1. Clinic services designed to provide medical and follow-up care for the infants, monitoring of development, and reinforcement of parental training will be made available on an outpatient basis at the hospital and in three satellite locations at hospitals from which the infants were initially transferred. See Appendix ___, which presents letters of agreement from the cooperating hospitals.

2. Prior to discharge of the infants and as much in advance as possible, the parents of eligible infants will be apprised of the program. They will be expected to complete most of the training before the infants are discharged. The program will be presented in such a manner as to relieve parental anxiety and facilitate parental bonding. The parents will be oriented to their infants' special needs and encouraged to participate in their care. The program form is designed to allow for flexible use of facilities, and it is expected to take about a month for the average parent to complete.

The parents will have access to 10 two-hour video tapes presenting simulated problem situations and solutions in real-life settings on the following subjects:

a. Nurturing, stimulation, exercise, and infection control in the home.
b. Special emergency conditions facing infants and signs of distress and what to do, including CPR and antichoking maneuvers.
c. Infant development and how to monitor for delays.
d. Availability of clinic follow-up care: what it is for and how to use it to best advantage.

Each clinic location will have a set of video viewers and tapes. Weekly group sessions will provide time for questions with staff members, hands-on training such as for CPR, and support from other parents.

The parents will be encouraged to make use of hospital meeting rooms for ongoing support groups.

To reach the educational objectives that the parents/caregivers acquire the knowledge necessary for the behavioral objectives, the following will be done:

3. The video tapes will be produced by the video arts faculty of ____ College, which is closely related to the ____ Hospital, having provided collaborative help in the past. Dr. ____, Director of Pediatrics, Dr. ____, Director of Patient Education, and rep-resentatives of the parents, reflecting the ethnic and educational range among the parents, will be involved in selection of content, manner of presentation, and initial fielding of the videos.

4. In addition to video tapes, workbooks will be prepared for home reference, utilizing existing material and with sections designed for the special needs of the parents. This will be the responsibility of the NICU nursing director in conjunction with the director of patient education.

Methods for the Process Objectives

The following describes the methods by which the targeted products will be produced and the milestones to be reached that will enable the project objectives to be reached.

continued

Participants in the project will include hospital personnel, consulting faculty from the video arts and nursing departments of _____ College, and from seven to ten parents whose infants are concurrently in the NICU. The participation of these parents in the project design is expected to provide guidelines that will make the material offered relevant and useful. Parents with infants concurrently at the hospital's NICU, who would otherwise be too early to receive the training, are thus able to benefit from the program, while enormously contributing to its design.

5. The curriculum content for the educational program will be approved by the directors of pediatrics and pediatric nursing (senior staff) and faculty members at _____ College. The basic material has been collected, and final selection will be based on input from the nurses and patient educators assigned to the project.

6. Video tapes for use in the program will be ready for use in three or four languages and approved by a review committee including representatives of the target parent population. It is anticipated that the cameras and video viewers will be on loan to the project or will have been presented as contributions in kind by the manufacturers. See letters of agreement, Appendix __. The video arts faculty will work with the project staff and parents, using hospital and home settings, with dolls and infants as appropriate. Since the tapes will be done in English and redubbed in Spanish, French, and Korean, an attempt will be made to work with parents for whom these are first languages.

7. The staff will be trained to lead the discussion groups and will be evaluated by senior staff members. Senior staff members involved in curriculum design will guide the nursing and patient education staff to be assigned to the discussion groups. They will observe practice sessions with parents.

8. Outreach material describing the training and clinic services will be produced by the patient education staff, in conjunction with parents, who will help select the issues to address and the language and tone. Materials will be tried out before final approval.

9. Procedures for referral of parents to training and clinic services will be designed to reflect the eligibility criteria. These will be presented to the relevant administrators, who will ensure that the staff incorporates them for use in regular NICU admissions, discharge planning, and discharge procedures.

10. Clinic services will be available in each location according to the letters of agreement presented in Appendix __.

11. Record forms for use in data collection/evaluation will be designed. Behavioral pre- and post-tests using video simulation and paper-and-pencil knowledge tests will be designed and field tested under the supervision of the senior staff members responsible for curriculum design and evaluation. Multipurpose forms will reflect the data-collection needs of selection, referral, evaluation, and infant monitoring and will be geared to the regular needs of patient charting. The video tapes will be excerpted for use in simulation tests to measure the desired behaviors. Responses will be given in interviews or by use of paper-and-pencil tests. Some testing will involve acting-out

continued

procedures, such as CPR with models. Paper-and-pencil tests will be designed to pick up task-specific knowledge.

12. To ensure that 95 percent of the infants eligible to have caregivers trained will have one or more caregivers participate in the program, outreach materials will be designed to encourage involvement. Since the state law requires that all patients be adequately prepared for discharge, parents will be informed that adequate preparation for NICU discharge involves parent preparation.

To ensure that 80 percent of the parents complete it, the training will be planned as much in advance of discharge as possible. Parents will be invited to participate as soon as it is learned that there is a reasonable expectation of their infant's survival. Parents who have not completed the training will be followed up to see what can be done to ensure completion, including referrals to social services as needed.

13. The distribution of tapes and evaluation reports will be facilitated by compilation of a mailing list of all NICUs and announcements in the relevant journals. Distribution will be provided according to the guidelines arrived at with the funder.

Example 5: Development of Leadership by Women of Color in the Antiviolence Movement

METHODOLOGY/PROJECT DESCRIPTION

Introduction

The method proposed for this project is designed to enable the antiviolence movement to draw on its untapped resources among women of color. These women, once assured of the commitment to and appreciation of the basic value of their inclusion in the work, can impel the movement forward to reasonable hope for change.

The possibility of a diverse, antiracist movement to end violence against women does exist. This project is designed to tap the creativity, enthusiasm, and experience offered by women of color.

Task Force Development

Women of color who currently hold leadership roles in domestic violence and sexual assault programs indicate that under the form of organization known as a *task force* the members positively respond to the issues addressed by their statements of purpose.[2] This is a form that will be used in this project.

Task forces serve to institutionalize diversity by empowering traditionally underrepresented groups, while they support and nurture the leadership of women of color. Task forces break isolation by providing a forum for women of color to exchange ideas and concerns.

Currently, there are Women of Color Task Forces in twelve statewide organizations. The project staff will draw on the experiences of these task forces and of the National Coalition Against Domestic Violence and the National Coalition

continued

Against Sexual Assault and use existing material on task force development[3] to produce recommendations on the development of women of color task forces. These recommendations will be offered to each state coalition of domestic violence and sexual assault programs, by way of contact with a woman of color in each state. Appendix ___ provides a list of state contacts.

The recommendations will speak only generally about prior experiences of other women of color regarding what seems to be helpful and necessary in the development of successful task forces. The content of the recommendations will include a definition of what a task force does, the role of task forces in an organization's work, and suggestions about how to build statewide support.

The information will be offered for the consideration of women in the state groups in relation to their needs and the circumstances faced in the different states.

Technical Assistance

Technical assistance offered by the project staff will not be limited to developing task forces. It will also refine ways to work with women of color to end violence against women. Examples of such topics include creating culturally relevant models of intervention, working with and for children of color, designing strategies to overcome resistance from White women, and organizing cross-culturally to combat racism.

Currently, the sponsoring organization, ____, is besieged with requests for technical assistance. Other requests will be generated through the Women of Color Task Forces, individuals working with diverse populations, and the national coalitions.

In keeping with the philosophy that the way to strengthen a national movement is through networking and organizing, technical assistance requests will be filled by many women of color across the country, women who possess the skills, resources, and desire to be associated with the project. In this way the technical assistance methodology will serve as an information and referral function for women of color working in domestic violence and sexual assault programs.

This system for provision of technical assistance will lead to the development of a National Skills Bank of Women of Color in the antiviolence movement. This skills bank will be a unique resource, because the traditional notions of "skills" or "expertise" will be expanded to include women of color who have years of organizing experience but little formal education, and women who have created unique services without mainstream resource or support. In this way the uniqueness of the work that women of color have undertaken can be truly reflected in the first national directory by and about women of color.

A critical aspect of the skills bank will be the clearinghouse function. A listing of the literature on women of color and the resources available to enhance the work of women of color will be maintained. This information will be useful to any individual or organization interested in providing services that are multicultural and antiracist. The Clearinghouse for Women of Color will serve to fulfill the tremendous need for relevant material.

During the first project year the project staff will respond to 35 requests for technical assistance, of which half will be referred to a regional associate.[4]

continued

The skills bank will be developed and the clearinghouse will be organized and operational by the beginning of the second year.

Curriculum Development and Leadership Training

The project will undertake to develop and distribute the Women of Color Leadership Development Curriculum and offer training based upon it. This curriculum will be used in conjunction with the more general leadership curriculum[5] developed by the sponsoring organization. The training will specifically address leadership issues for women of color.

Exercises in the curriculum include: developing strategies for combatting racism, culturally relevant models of service delivery, leadership and organizing, and dealing with cultural differences among women of color.

Although specific topics included in the curriculum will relate to women of color working in the antiviolence movement, the themes will be generalizable to women of color who work in other areas. The format of the curriculum presentation will be similar to the work now being done with the existing curriculum.

The curriculum and training will be part of available project-conducted leadership development seminars, and will also be offered as a track in state conferences and as a separate activity. Outreach to inform the public of what is available will be done through state organizations, women of color task forces, and the organizations already receiving prior training by the sponsor.

Groups interested in the training will be asked to contact the project to negotiate costs, scheduling, and participation. The bases on which groups will be accepted, such as social class, sexual identity, region, accessibility, and commitment to the movement will be discussed and will enter into the final decisions on training. It has been the experience of the sponsor organization that this structured planning process is instructive for leadership training in and of itself.

9

Articulating the Basic Components
of the Proposal

SCHEMATIC LAYOUT OF THE BASIC COMPONENTS

It is almost impossible to remember to cover all the items you have in mind about problems, objectives, and methods without a schematic layout of the parts, showing their connections. Not only that, you may discover that there are gaps in the design that must be taken into account when filling in a layout of the project, and often new ideas come in response to the concentration required to do the exercise of creating the layout.

Layout Concepts

The process of designing the project and then writing about it requires an articulation of the components of problem, objectives, and methods. A schematic layout of the components is shown in Figure 9.1.

The problems are the reasons the project is undertaken, so there is a need to have a problem statement to which each project objective relates.

It is useful to write brief problem statements (without the support material) in outline form and then write the objectives that relate to the problems alongside the referent problems. This way you can insert the goals beside the broad problems and eventually write the theoretical statements beside the goals statements and see how these relate. The broad statement of method is really your hypothesis of what major methodological approach will achieve your ultimate goals. The methods sections are laid out beside the objectives and are numbered to correspond.

FIGURE 9.1
Basic Schematic Project Layout

PROBLEMS	OBJECTIVES	METHODS
Broad Problem	Long Range Goals/Objectives	Theoretical Statement
Contributing Problem(s)	Project Objectives: Broad/Behavioral	Project Methods
	Related Process Objectives	Related Methods
Educational (Intermediary) Problems	Project Objectives: Educational/Intermediary	Project Methods
	Related Process Objectives	Related Methods

The broad problem and goals lead to contributing problems and project (behavioral) objectives, for which the major aspects of your project are the methods. These generate process objectives having to do with setting up the project, which in turn call for methods statements.

The behavioral objectives, which relate to changes in what the target population will do or conditions that will change, generate educational objectives (if you have an educational method), the content of which you have hypothesized will lead to the behavioral change.

Educational objectives have methods dealing with the educational techniques, and their related process objectives deal with the production of curriculum, creation of instructional materials, and other products or milestones to be produced by given dates. These, in turn, also have methods.

The other benefit of doing a schematic layout is that it enormously simplifies the process of writing the actual sections of the proposal. There is a logical outline ready, and the parts can be shifted at will, with nothing lost in the way of detail.

When this scheme is followed it is easy to see how adding a new objective should be followed through with a corresponding problem statement, if not already included, and a methods statement, which in turn may generate new process objectives and process objective methods. It is also easy to see where objectives belong in the logical sequence. If the due dates are included, it is also easier to arrange the methods section in order of due dates when you are ready to do so.

Example

Exhibit 10 is an example of a schematic project layout. You may notice that the problem, objectives, and methods statements in this layout were changed to some extent by the time they appeared in the final sections shown in Exhibits 7, 8, and 9. This is natural, because the final writing is a refinement of the work that has gone before. The schematic layout is really your set of notes, making for easy revision and articulation of the parts.

EXHIBIT 10
Example of Basic Schematic Project Layout: Education of Parents of Infants Discharged from Intensive Care

PROBLEMS	OBJECTIVES	METHODS
Broad Problem Slowing of decline in infant mortality; continued high rates for Blacks and minorities. 1. Gains in neonatal rates not matched in post-neonatal mortality. 2. High risk of morbidity and developmental delays for low birth weight post neonatal survivors.	**Long Range Goals/Objectives** Accelerated decline in infant mortality; parity in Black/White rates. By 18 mos. post discharge: 1. Gains in survival rates for infants discharged from NICU whose care-givers receive pre/post-discharge training and follow-up clinic care. 2. Decline in morbidity and developmental delays for infants discharged from NICU whose caregivers receive pre/post-discharge training and follow-up clinic care.	**Theoretical Statement** The project offers a method to reduce the morbidity and mortality among graduates of infant intensive care units, with emphasis on poverty and minority families. It should reduce postneonatal mortality and morbidity and thereby, the infant mortality rate. An educational project addressed to mothers and other caregivers pre-discharge, and provision of follow-up clinic services is offered.
Contributing Problem(s) 3. Infants from impoverished homes receive little follow-up care. 4. Many young, poorly educated parents are not able to provide: a. Appropriate parenting b. Proper response to emergencies c. Appropriate monitoring of developmental delays	**Behavioral Objectives** By the end of 30 months into the project period: 3. 80 percent of infants whose caregivers receive pre-discharge training will be regularly attending a follow-up clinic. 4. Caregivers will display a. Appropriate parenting b. Proper response to emergencies c. Appropriate monitoring of developmental delays	**Project Methods** 3. Clinic services designed to monitor and care for the infants and reinforce training. 4. Predischarge training covering: a. Nurturing, stimulation, exercise, infection control geared to home conditions.

continued

PROBLEMS	OBJECTIVES	METHODS
		b. Special emergency conditions facing infants; signs of distress/what to do, including CPR, anti-choking maneuvers. c. Infant development; how to monitor for developmental delays.
	<u>Related Process Objectives</u> By the end of the 7th month of the project: a. Clinic services available. b. Procedures for referral to training and clinic services in place. c. Record forms for use in data collection/evaluation in place. d. Outreach material describing the training and clinic services ready for use. e. Training program on stream.	<u>Related Methods</u> a. Incorporation of new content into existing out-pt. facilities; adding rooms for counseling, VCR viewing; transfer of appropriate staff. b. Referral criteria designed based on weight at birth, severity of initial illness, length of time in NICU, economic status/education of mother, home situation; with inputs from pediatric and nursing directors. c. Examination of evaluation design, referral needs, reporting requirements, future research needs, and current records to provide multipurpose forms d. Patient education staff, in conjunction with current parent representatives decide issues to address, language and tone. Tryouts before adoption.

continued

EXHIBIT 10, continued

PROBLEMS	OBJECTIVES	METHODS
Educational (Intermediary) Problems 5. Mothers and other care-givers lack knowledge of special caregiving needs of the infants after dis-charge, do not know about emergencies and emergency care, nor about the con-tent or need to monitor for developmental delays.	Project Objectives: Educational/Intermediary 5. Upon completion of the training, caregivers will demonstrate a post-test knowledge of: a. The need for continued clinic follow up b. Parenting/nurturing for NICU graduates c. Procedures in case of emergencies d. Infant development, pos-sible delays, how to spot them, and what to do.	Project Methods 5. The curriculum will cover the areas needed to bring about the desired behavioral objectives. The form used will be video-taped lessons utiliz-ing real situations either simulated or actual. All the mater-ial will be covered on tape. In addition to work books, discussion groups will be avail-able once per week. Rooms with VCRs will be available so parents can study at convenient times. An estimated 10 2-hour tapes, plus 4 group sessions will be needed pre-discharge. Average of one month. The tapes will be redubbed in the lan-guages characteristic to the catchment area: Spanish, French and Korean (perhaps). More to be added as needed. The tapes will be copied and made avail-able at the clinic.
	Related Process Objectives f. Curriculum content for the project will be ap-proved by the end of the first month. g. Video tapes and the work book will be ready for use by the end of the 7th month in 3 languages. h. Pre/post behavioral tests based on video simulation and knowledge tests using paper and pencil response will be ready by the end of the 7th month. i. Staff will be trained to lead the discussion groups by the end of the seventh month. j. By the end of the first 30 months of the project	Related Methods f. The basic material has been collected; final selection will be determined by the senior staff in col-laboration with fac-ulty in nursing and pt. education from _____ College. g. The video arts facul-ty will work with the project staff and parent volunteers in the filming, using hospital and home settings, with dolls or infants, as appro-priate. Parents and community people have agreed to help with

continued

EXHIBIT 10, continued

PROBLEMS	OBJECTIVES	METHODS
	90 percent of those eligible for the training will be active in the program, and 80% will be successfully completing it. k. Tapes and program materials will be available for distribution to interested NICUs, together with the first evaluation results by the end of the 31st mo.	the translations. h. The pre/post tests will be designed by senior staff and filmed by the video team using the same players and/or sections of the lesson tapes; parent volunteers will be used to ensure reading/writing compatibility of tests w/target population. i. Staff will be trained by senior staff involved in curriculum design.

10

Significance

TYPES OF SIGNIFICANCE

Significance for the Funding Agency's Interests

In various sections of the proposal the funding agency expects you to make a case for the significance of your project. The first is in relation to the funding agency's interests. You establish this by showing how the project will accomplish the purpose(s) of the request for proposal, request for application, or statement of the funding agency's programmatic aims and criteria.

In the case of foundations you may wish to quote from the published policy statement and then elaborate on the way your project addresses the issues. For federal funding it is often enough to indicate the part of the RFA to which you are responding. But it is always useful to elaborate further.

The statement of significance in relation to the funding agency's interests can be part of the introduction or part of a section on significance. It is also needed in the letter of transmittal — with proposals for which such letters, rather than cover form sheets, are appropriate. At least one federal agency requires that the number and letter of the particular section of the offering plan to which the applicant is responding be identified in the applicant's letter of transmittal.

This aspect of significance has been covered at the beginning of Chapter 5 and will not be elaborated further here.

Significance of the Problem, Significance of the Method

The significance of the problem is established in the problem statement. The significance of the method is established when you compare your selection of method with what else is going on in the field, the state of the art, and your review of the literature. These are usually presented in the sections mentioned and were covered in Chapters 6 and 8. They are rarely placed as separate sections, but if need be they can be taken out of those sections and elaborated on separately.

Significance of the Project: Wider Impact

Significance as a separate topic usually means the impact of the program, that is, the wider benefits going beyond those immediately measurable under project objectives. For instance, there may be effects on persons related to the target population, such as the employers who will benefit as the result of an educational program. An effect beyond the immediate objectives for the target population might be an improvement in student grades as a result of an arts program. There may be changes in social or administrative attitudes or structures. A project may encourage a shift of emphasis from purely medical solutions to social solutions; the role of patient education may be increased; nurses facing burnout may be heartened by improved outcomes; a school system may consider other ways of taking students outside their local communities for curriculum enrichment.

The impact may have to do with other problems of the target population or other related behaviors. For example, the educational experience may result in encouragement of parents to study more; employers may be encouraged to use the arts model as a basis for career explorations in their industry. A research project may foster a new way of thinking about related problems in the field.

Chances for Success

The likelihood of the success of a methodology is enormously enhanced if the target population has had the opportunity to help design the program and supports it. Participation of the target population in choosing the problem, method, or objectives enhances the project's significance. This should influence the way you set about to design the project, and if you do involve representatives of the target population, you can refer to that in a section on significance.

Model for Others

Your project will be considered significant if it paves the way for others, that is, if it will make it possible for others to replicate what you have done or to build on what you have accomplished. For example, provision of final reports that include the results of evaluation design, production of curricula and/or instructional materials that others will be able to use, or addition of a documented, scientific link in a chain that will ultimately lead to an important breakthrough are all indications of significance. (Being a replicable model is sometimes the meaning given to "wider impact.")

WRITING THE SECTION ON SIGNIFICANCE

You should decide what ways your project is significant and include a statement about each in a separate section on significance, assuming that the agency's instructions do not specify the details of a section on significance. Remember never to repeat your section on objectives as a substitute for the statement of significance.

A DISCUSSION/CONCEPT PAPER

The introduction, problem, objectives, methods, and significance sections can become the basis of a discussion paper used to solicit critical comments from potential funding sources, from in-house senior staff members in your agency, and from potential supporters. Even if they are not needed for those purposes, it is a good idea to write these sections well ahead of the others, allowing time to assimilate, review, and revise before the evaluation design and other sections are tackled. Exhibit 11 presents three examples of significance statements.

EXHIBIT 11
Examples of Statements on Significance

Example 2: Ambulance Staff Training in Emergency Medical Services

SIGNIFICANCE

No emergency medical service anywhere in the United States today has a procedure in place for the prehospital administration of clot-dissolving agents to heart attack victims. This project provides an opportunity to successfully demonstrate a method of

continued

having paramedics administer streptokinase in the field, and thus establish a model that can be utilized by other emergency medical service systems nationwide.

By disseminating the results of the data we collect, we can help in the eventual reduction of mortality and morbidity resulting from heart attacks, not only in the catchment area of the hospital but throughout the city, state, and nation.

Example 3: City Children Involved in the Arts Community

SIGNIFICANCE

The project is a pilot study that can open the way to reaching students throughout the city in an expanded program. The periodic project reports, sharing the project experience and the evaluation data, will make it possible for the project model to be tried in other communities; it has the potential of serving as a national model for cities with resident arts neighborhoods.

The isolation of artists from the educational process, which has been commented on in the literature,[9] can begin to be reversed. The cooperation of the city's board of education is making it possible for inner-city students to leave their neighborhoods for curriculum enrichment. This can lead the way to other cooperative ventures between the schools and the arts community.

The model can also be adapted for other fields, such as the business and scientific communities, where experiences of work and finding out what it is like to engage in particular occupations could widen the career horizons of young people.

The impact of the project goes beyond the enrichment of the students and the possibility of inspiring some youngsters to enter the art world. Opening up to creative expression has demonstrated elsewhere[10] that grades improve when the students feel the interest of teachers and role models.

The project also offers a chance to provide, if only in a minor way, for art-related income for artists by involving them in teaching, thus giving them a way to further explore their art through teaching and exchange.

The world of art itself will benefit from the impact on the artists who will be opening their creative experiences to these youth and their world. New ideas and new sensibilities can be expected to emerge in the fields of visual arts, dance, and theater as the experiences are assimilated and the artists continue to work.

Example 4: Writing Skills for Retention of Graduate Students

SIGNIFICANCE

The success of the project is predictable from the current interest expressed by the target population: candidates for admission into the participating graduate programs whom we have to turn down because of their writing, and students unable to maintain 3.0+ grade point averages when writing is included in the grading. These students and potential students ask for remedial classes, only to be told that any undergraduate classes in writing have heavy waiting lists, are reserved for undergraduates, or do not provide training adequate to meet graduate writing standards.

continued

The impact of the program goes beyond the students themselves. It will allow them to enter graduate programs that will advance them professionally. The programs involved are in the social services and health, including occupations in short supply of effectively trained individuals, such as nursing, allied health services administration, social service workers, urban planners, and professionals in environmental control. These vital occupations stand to gain as more individuals with less than optimal educational preparation learn to write well enough to obtain graduate degrees. The jobs that they will fill will be steps on career ladders, and therefore attractive to the new arrivals. This can only enhance the quality of job performance and job stability in these occupations.

The model will be available for other disciplines, such as in the arts and humanities, wherever prior undergraduate writing standards are not adequate to equip students who aspire to work at the graduate level. The project is another step to providing access to and retention in graduate study for individuals with English as a second language or inadequate writing preparation, who need help if we are to say we provide quality education for all.

11

Evaluation Design

After you are clear about the objectives and methods you will propose, you are ready to prepare for the evaluation section of the proposal. This chapter and Chapter 12 are designed to give you most of the guidance you will need in writing the evaluation section of the proposal. However, it is a good idea to supplement this with a reference text on statistics or evaluation. (See the evaluation section of the Selected Bibliography.)

The evaluation section is the most technically demanding part of project planning. But remember, you have the expertise of colleagues to draw on, and not all projects will require the experimental or quasi-experimental design that you will read about here. As you read, remember, too, that Chapter 12 deals with writing and has examples.

The most important thing about evaluation design is that a good design fits the objectives. Once you state an objective properly, good design should follow. The evaluation design is a statement made *now* about what you will do during the funding period to assess the success of the project. You will be answering the following questions:

1. How will you prove that the project objectives are met?

2. How will you monitor operations to ensure that the project activities and the products promised are being delivered properly?

3. For each objective, how will you define and measure success?

4. Will you compare your results with comparison group(s), with the subject group at an earlier time, according to an objective standard, or with any other criteria?

5.   What data will you collect? When? By whom? In what form? What method of analysis?

6.   What use will you make of the results?

Proposals are asked to include evaluation design because funders want to be sure you will be able to prove your success by the end of the funding period. Even if the guidelines do not specifically call for an evaluation design, you will have a competitive edge if you include one. The evaluation design says you will be responsible for your results.

TYPES OF EVALUATION

Much evaluation theory recognizes three types of evaluation: evaluation research, project evaluation, and process evaluation. A description of each will help you match the type of evaluation to the type of objective. (See Table 1.1, part III, which presents evaluation types related to project types.)

Evaluation Research
(summative: relates to project objectives)

Evaluation research is also called clinical trial or program trial. It is used for formal hypothesis testing and applies when a method or treatment is being tested. Experimental design is most desirable, but quasi-experimental design is acceptable in education, administration, and service programs.

Answers

The questions evaluation research must answer are, Did I get the results I predicted? Did my method account for the results? Under what conditions can I expect such results? The design must be rigorous; the object is to add knowledge to the field.

Likely Features

The most likely features of evaluation research are scientific method, random assignment to test and control groups, multivariate analysis, a theoretical basis, and a concern with making generalizations not only to the target population but beyond. (These terms are explained later.) The results are written with publication in mind.

Project Evaluation
(summative: relates to project objectives)

Project evaluation is appropriate for a demonstration grant, assessment of the operation of a service, or generalization about the success of a proven method to the specific project situation. Experimental design is desirable, but quasi-experimental designs are acceptable.

Answers

The questions a project evaluation must answer are, Did I get the results I predicted? and Did my method account for the results? The design must be rigorous enough to justify conclusions leading to a continuation of the method or moving on to the next developmental stage.

Likely Features

The most likely features of a project evaluation are nonrandom or random assignment to test and control groups, use of simple analysis and comparisons, and concern with showing effectiveness in the project situation. The results may be written for publication or made available to others.

Process Evaluation
(formative: relates to process objectives)

Process evaluation is appropriate for projects that have products and milestone objectives, and for pilot tests. When used as project monitoring, it applies to *all* projects.

Answers

The questions a process evaluation must answer are, Did I deliver the products, milestone activities, and main project activities I promised to deliver in the quality, quantity, and time frame promised? For pilot tests, Did I find the "bugs" in the idea?

The design of a process evaluation is generally not more complicated than a check to make sure due dates, targets for outreach, attendance, and other numbers were met and that the quality of the products has been approved by experts. For the development of research instruments, questionnaires, and data collection, however, statistical standards of reliability and validity should be used and demonstrated. For project monitoring, you might include collection of data on client satisfaction, employee performance evaluation, and financial and benefit/cost analyses.

Likely Features

The most likely features of process evaluation are comparison of performance with predetermined standards of quality and quantity and a check to see if the due dates are met. The most significant feature of a process evaluation, since it is formative, is that you are expected to correct the problems it uncovers *during* the course of the project. The results are presented in progress reports to the funding agency.

SUCCESS CRITERIA

A *success criterion* is a point or standard on a dimension or variable that is the minimum level you promise to reach as a measure of your attainment of an objective. You name a rate or score on some form of measurement. Examples are reaching a neonatal death rate of 6.6 deaths per 1,000 live births, achieving Black/White parity of infant mortality rates, reaching 90 percent class attendance, having 90 percent achieve scores of 85 percent or better on a test of knowledge, obtaining a favorable review from a known authority for a curriculum design, or finishing construction of a facility by a given date.

The following language is relevant to project evaluation design: With regard to project objectives, the method you are evaluating is referred to as the *treatment* (a statistical term), or the *intervention*.

The group of people you are studying in the evaluation design will probably be a subset of all those getting the intervention. They are the *test group,* or the *subject sample.* If you are looking at managerial functioning you may have a *test,* or *subject,* department or time period.

If you are using a group of people not receiving the treatment, or receiving another treatment for comparisons, they are a *control group* if randomly selected and assigned to the test or control group. They are a *comparison group* if selected in some other way.

You will want to collect data about the situation as it is before the intervention. These are called *baseline data,* or *pretest data.* Similar data collected after the intervention is over are called *posttest data.* In this context the term "test" does not necessarily mean that the baseline data were the result of taking a test. Any type of measure could be called pre- or post-test data.

In your evaluation design you take each objective and state it with your selected success criterion, your projected measure of success. You not only predict the general quality you will achieve but how much — how good. So in the parent-education program, you may have a checklist of activities you say the parents must be carrying out at a point in time. You may start with baseline data on the compliance on the part of the test group and on the part of the comparison group. You will want to show an improvement after your project's intervention in the test group as compared with the comparison group. For example, your criterion might be that after the intervention test-group attendance at a clinic is 20 percent higher than the attendance of the comparison group. You may select a specific level of improvement (at least one visit per month) or a statistically significant increase.

Your success criterion is a quantitative point on a standard measuring scale against which you compare the results you actually obtain. You set the criterion high enough to be a clearly desirable point, but not so high you will fail. Your selection of the standard against which to compare is determined by the nature of your objective and the instruments provided in the literature or designed by you.

Sources from which you may wish to select criteria are given under the headings that follow.

Preestablished Normative Data

You may use already existing norms with which to compare your group's data or results. For instance, Graduate Record Examination scores and laboratory blood tests have been normed against known populations, and any score can be interpreted in terms of the distribution of the standard scores. In such a case you must know whether your population can fairly be compared with the one on which the test was normed.

An Absolute Standard

To use an absolute standard, you predict what percentage of 100 your group will reach. No allowance is made for distribution data, because success is not relative. An example of this kind of standard is an exam with a cut-off score for passing or failing, such as the written portion of a driving test.

A Theoretical Standard

Reports in the literature on the type of outcome for a similar program can supply a theoretical standard. You make a reasonable prediction based on what has happened elsewhere. One such application would be predicting an improved smoking cessation rate compared with what has been achieved elsewhere, given the method.

Goal-Attainment Scaling

When the dimensions of change must be identified individually and separately for each subject, the source of your criteria can be derived by goal-attainment scaling. An instance of this would be predicting the degree of independence of handicapped persons after a program to promote self-sufficiency. Scales are constructed for each activity, such as dressing, shopping, cooking, communicating, and physical mobility. The scale points are descriptions of increasing competence levels of the activity. The scales should be constructed using the technique of equal appearing intervals (see Edwards in selected bibliography). Upon entry into the program, each subject is rated on the scales (the pretest) by an expert in the field. The expert assesses the subject professionally and rates him or her for current level of functioning, plus where that subject would be with the program intervention and without. At the end, an expert again rates the subjects, and the results are compared with the earlier predictions. This technique allows for weighted composite scores for individuals and groups and can be used to compare test and comparison groups.

Public Health Data for Population Groups

Pre- and post-test comparisons may be made with Census or health data for a given area, sex or age group to show favorable change in the test group. The assumption is that the test group is only a small part of the population group and that any difference is due to the intervention. A specific instance of this would be comparing test-group pregnancy rates by age and race with Census data for the area in the same age and race categories.

A Published Standard Met by a Broader Population

An example of this is arriving at parity with data for the White population by a minority group. This is similar to the use of public health data for population groups in general.

Legal Requirements

Standards are set by licensure or accreditation agencies, such as cut-offs on licensure exams or sanitation or environmental standards set by law.

Pretest/Posttest

Where the criterion is comparison of a posttest with a pretest, the test group is predicted to show a percentage or absolute improvement over its own baseline scores.

Control or Comparison Group

With a control or comparison group the test group is predicted to do better than a comparable group that gets no treatment or a different treatment. Pre- and post-testing may also be involved.

Expert Assessment

The criterion may be analysis by a known expert who judges the outcome for quality based on professional standards, as in curriculum evaluation or review of a literary product. While subjective, predetermined evaluation categories or a global rating can be used.

One of the more challenging issues in the areas of health, education, social service, and management is to design success criteria for behavioral objectives. It is fairly straightforward to measure by death rates, profit rates, and other broad-objective criteria. It is also fairly simple to measure changes in knowledge and attitudes for intermediary objectives. In health education in particular, much data collected *are* knowledge and attitude scores. But we do not know whether success in changing knowledge or attitudes leads to changes in the behaviors that are the true program objectives. There are few measures of behavior other than self-reporting.

How do we measure patient compliance or changes in management style, sexual practice, eating habits, stress control? Unless these behavioral objectives can be measured, we cannot know whether intermediary-level interventions are effective. That is *your* challenge: to find stand-in measures for the behaviors. The instruments must be able to produce data that are repeatable and stable, that is, *statistically reliable,* and they must also be good approximations for the actual measure you would like to have, that is, *statistically valid.*

DESIGN CONSIDERATIONS

Comparisons

For project evaluation you may want to make pretest comparisons of the control and test groups to show that they are comparable before the intervention; pretest/posttest comparisons of the test and control groups to show a change in the posttest for the test group; and comparison of pre- and post-test changes in the two groups to demonstrate that the size of the change is greater for the test group.

In each case, in order to specify the success criterion, you must name the test instrument or standard you will use and specify the magnitude of the results that will be considered successful. Each objective can now be stated with an ending phrase, "as measured by," where you state the change criterion and name the measuring instrument.

All this also implies a plan for the nature of the data and whether and when you will select groups, collect data, and run your analysis. Together, these become the evaluation design.

Moderator Variables

Moderator variables are conditions, events, and characteristics that can affect the outcome you are trying to influence by your intervention. They are of concern because we wish to attribute the results solely to our intervention and they "get in the way." We wish to show that the results are due to the intervention and not other events and forces, or at least to show what part was due to the intervention.

Much of evaluation design is devoted to finding ways in which to account for the "confounding variables" or "moderator variables" so that the results can be unambiguously interpreted. Variables that can affect the outcomes can be special characteristics of the population served, of the staff, of the environment, or of the way the intervention is delivered.

External, non-project-specific moderator variables are dealt with in evaluation design by application of statistically based concepts, described as follows:

Internal validity describes the extent to which an observed effect (criterion) can be attributed to the planned intervention (treatment). There may be competing explanations for the results. The main threats to internal validity are explained in the following pages.

External validity describes the extent to which an observed effect can be generalized to other settings and populations with similar characteristics but without the experimental conditions. This will also be explained.

Factors Affecting Internal Validity and Ways to Deal with Them

History: Outside Events

Unpredictable, singular occurrences in the social or physical environment can have a widespread effect on the criterion measure; such an occurrence might be a new advertising campaign on smoking dangers or a statement by a famous person about breast self-examination.

Solution: A randomly selected control group or comparison group that is also subject to these events is selected. Both groups have the same exposure during the time period, and there are pre- and post-test data for both. (*Random selection* means that everyone in the target population has an equal chance of being selected to be in each test group, and assignment to either the test or control group is also random. Assignments with less rigor produce comparison groups.)

History: Secular Trend

Influences over time can affect the subjects in a steady direction and affect the results for all the subjects. For example, social pressures influence long-term changes in rates of breast feeding; there is gradual public acceptance of exercise; and there are changing attitudes about smoking.

Solution: Use a control group, or have several pretests in time series and compute the secular trend so it can be subtracted from posttest results.

Maturation

Subjects may change in the direction predicted due to natural effects of aging or socialization, as with loss of embarrassment with experience, improvement in physical skills in the young as they mature, and decreased numbers of sexual partners with aging.

Solution: Use a control group, or employ time series (consecutive sampling) in pretests and posttests to determine a maturation trend line. (This is similar to the way to deal with a secular trend.)

Testing Effects

Subjects may learn from taking the pretest (practice effect), or their consciousness is affected by having to think about the test material; being observed or measured affects the outcome.

Solution: Have two test and two control groups. One test and one control group get both pre- and posttests; one test and one control group get only the posttest. Analysis of variance can isolate the contributions of each factor.

Instrumentation

Pre- and posttests may not measure the same thing, or test conditions may vary with respect to factors such as fatigue of subjects, attitude of tester, type of test conditions, time, and duration of the test.

Solution: Use posttests only for at least one test group and one control group, or establish the test/retest reliability of the tests and conditions and enforce uniform conditions.

Statistical Regression: Convergence to the Mean

Extreme measures tend to disappear in posttesting, affecting the results.

Solution: Have large enough samples to do analysis with and without outliers (and their matched pairs if any); use a series of test groups.

Selection Bias

The comparison group may not be equivalent to the treatment group with respect to important variables. Self-selected treatment groups and other convenience samples may have characteristics that predict success or failure.

Solution: Assign subjects randomly to treatment and control groups; or use matched pairs when key variables are known; and use pretest data to establish the comparability of the groups.

Participant Attrition

Subjects who drop out create bias. Since dropouts tend not to be randomly distributed, they systematically affect the results.

Solution: Use matched pairs. When a subject leaves, the counterpart in the control group is also dropped. Use a series of test groups so that other, later groups can be compared.

Contamination Effects

Controls can be influenced by the program through exposure to the treatment group, or the program may affect the way a control group is treated.

Solution: Choose controls in an institution where contact is unlikely.

Factors Affecting External Validity: Reactive Effects of Testing

Interaction of Experimental Conditions with Methods (Hawthorne Effect). Being in a special situation makes everyone try harder. Paying *any* kind of attention, not just applying the treatment, improves outcomes.

Social Desirability Effect. Subjects want to please the evaluator.

Placebo Effect. Belief that the treatment will work produces the desired results.

Novelty Effect. A transitory capturing of the subjects' attention can give good results, followed by a later falling off as the novelty fades.

Pygmalion Effect. The teacher or treatment giver's expectations affect the outcome.

Solutions

Control Groups. Single blind: subject cannot tell which is treatment, which placebo. Double blind: subject and provider do not know who gets placebo. Triple blind: evaluators, provider, and subjects do not know.

Serial Posttesting or Delayed Posttesting. Serial posttesting and delayed posttesting pick up sleeper effects (delayed improvements) or falling off effects (delayed decline in improvement) by making trends obvious.

Unobtrusive Measuring Techniques.

Project-Specific Moderator Variables

Project-specific moderator variables are variables that are determined from the context of the project situation. For example, the postneonatal mortality rates for neonatal intensive care graduates will be influenced by weight at birth, severity of initial illness, and the mothers' health, whether or not the parent training takes place. We expect to modify the results but can only find out how much when we know how important the other factors are. The success of students in a writing class will be affected by the level of skills they come in with. Whether the staff speaks the same language as the target population may affect the outcome. Whether a student has access to study space and quiet may affect grades.

Evaluation design can deal with project-specific variables by holding them constant for all participants in the program, as in studying only poor, Black women between the ages of 20 to 30; but there is a resulting inability to generalize beyond the specific variables held constant. The full range of variables can be represented systematically in the subject and comparison groups, allowing for subgroup analysis. You can match the test and comparison groups on the variables, or you can measure the contribution of moderator variables by measuring them for each participant and performing multivariate analysis. As an example, to evaluate a writing course, you might do multiple correlation analysis including attendance in the class (the intervention); pre- and post-test grades for writing (the criterion variable); and age, sex, grade point average, income level, and study time.

It is up to you to identify the relevant project-specific moderator variables. You can consult the literature and/or use common sense. Then you arrange to control for them and describe this in your proposal.

Ways to Control for Project-Specific Moderator Variables: A Summary

1. Have a large enough random sample to do subgroup analysis.
2. Match the groups on the key value ranges of the variables.
3. Stratify on the variables.
4. Measure the variables and include them in multivariate analysis such as correlation analysis, analysis of variance, and factor analysis, so as to account for their contribution to the results.
5. Control for variables by selecting a homogeneous sample with respect to them, but realize that no generalization can be made beyond the characteristics of the sample population.

EXPERIMENTAL DESIGN

Experimental design takes account of many moderator variables by setting up rigorous conditions. It requires posttest observation after the treatment; the test group is chosen at random; there is a control group; there is pretest observation before the intervention; and the subjects are randomly assigned to the test or control groups.

In a *probability sample* every subject in a predefined population has an equal chance of being included in the study. In a *convenience sample* the population is defined by those available. Random samples may be *simple, systematic* (the first subject is selected at random, and then every *n*th one is selected from an unorganized pool), *stratified* (the population is first divided by some salient characteristics such as sex or age, and then random selection is taken from each stratum in a representative fashion), or *cluster* (groupings such as houses, streets, wards, and classes are randomly selected, but each unit in a selected grouping is included).

Elements of Experimental Design

1. Posttest observation after treatment.
2. Representative (probability) sample, that is, with random selection and equal opportunity to be selected.
3. Use of at least one control group (randomly selected).
4. Pretest observation before treatment and for at least one control group.
5. Random assignment to treatment and control groups.

Internal Validity

For greatest internal validity, in descending order of preference, use

1. All five elements of experimental design.
2. A convenience sample with random assignment.
3. Random selection; no pretests.
4. A convenience sample; no pretests; random assignment.
5. A matched comparison group.
6. A matched comparison group; no pretests.
7. Random selection; no controls.
8. A convenience sample, no controls.
9. Random selection; no controls; no pretest.
10. A convenience sample; no controls; no pretest.

External Validity

For greatest external validity, in descending order of preference, use

1. All five elements of experimental design.
2. No pretests; random selection.
3. Matched controls; random selection.
4. No controls; random selection.
5. No pretest; no controls; random selection.
6. A convenience sample.
7. No pretest; convenience sample.
8. Matched controls; convenience sample.
9. No controls; convenience sample.
10. No pretest; no controls; convenience sample.

QUASI-EXPERIMENTAL ALTERNATIVES

While experimental design is attractive for the problems it solves, the world of finite resources, practical considerations, ethics, and the complexities of nonlaboratory conditions results in compromise. Systematic nonrandom assignment to comparison groups, testing of the subject group serially over time instead of having controls, comparison of several test groups over several cycles rather than a control group at the same point in time, and use of goal-attainment scaling rather than uniform test instruments — are all acceptable, quasi-experimental alternatives.

In making decisions the evaluation designer is asked to choose the design that distorts the conclusions least. That means knowing which variables are likely to affect the outcome the most, and therefore most confuse the results. Knowing which ones to "control" requires knowledge of the subject matter and the literature, and also requires creative insight.

Only in the case of clinical or program trial are the standards so rigorous as to be beyond the grasp of an average intelligent professional.

Ethical considerations may make withholding of a treatment from the control group repugnant. One solution is *staging*. A treatment and a control group are selected. After the posttest is completed, the control group receives the treatment. The posttest then serves as the second pretest for the control group, which is now the second treatment group. This can go on. If all the groups continue to be tested, this also provides time-series data.

An elaborate example of staging can be done in a situation where there is a large number in the population to receive the treatment and facilities permit only a few at a time to receive it. An example might be a large staff to receive training in prevention of abuse of clients in a facility to care for the handicapped. The staging could proceed as follows:

The basic design would include staged use of test and comparison groups, so that there is a group receiving training and one without training for four training cycles, with the comparison group being trained subsequent to its function as a control. This is illustrated in Figure 11.1. For each group except Group 1 there are two pretests and a posttest. During the period between the two pretests, each group serves as a comparison group for the group preceding it in training. The second pretest is also the group's posttest while it is serving as a control. In this way the test and comparison groups are in the same time period, controlling for history. Group 1 has only one pretest, and Group 5 has no posttest after training if no other test group will follow. There are four test groups in this design and four comparison groups, even though only five groups are actually involved, and each group is trained.

This design can also accommodate random assignment to groups, assuming that everyone will eventually be trained, and there is no need to select trainees by block, as, for example, by department. Alternatively, the effect of contamination can be taken care of by selecting the groups so that they are located in the institution far from their matched group.

FIGURE 11.1
Example of Training/Comparison Group Staging

	Time 1	Time 2	Time 3	Time 4	Time 5
Group 1	X ———— X				
Group 2	X	X ———— X			
Group 3		X	X ———— X		
Group 4			X	X ———— X	
Group 5				X	X —— etc.

Key: ———— training intervention
  X   pre/test; post/test

DESCRIBING THE RESULTS

Descriptive statistics tell about the distribution of a single trait in a population in measures such as a mean or standard deviation, or the relationship of two or more traits in a population, such as the coefficient of correlation. These measures are appropriate under any circumstances. If you study everyone in a given population, you are not concerned with whether your sample is like the population; you are studying the population. Your conclusions apply to that population but cannot be generalized beyond it. That may be all you need.

Inferential statistics draw conclusions about a population from data collected through a sample. Measures are needed to judge whether an observed result can be attributed to random errors introduced when the sample was drawn.

Statistical significance tests the degree to which the results can be attributed to chance sampling error. This is appropriate only when probability sampling has been done. However, any errors introduced through self-selection and other threats to validity are not random and are not dealt with through tests of significance.

The strength of the measure of association, or the magnitude of the relationship, is an essential measure for all evaluations. Such measures include lambda for nominal data, gamma for ordinal data, and the coefficient of correlation for interval or ratio variables.

When there is probability sampling, you will be testing the significance between sample means on pre- and posttests of the treatment group, pre- and posttests of the controls, pretest/pretest comparison of the treatment and controls to establish comparability, posttest/posttest comparison of the treatment and control groups, and pretest/posttest comparison of the differences between the treatment and control groups (all using *t*-test data, tests of the statistical significance of differences between sample means).

.   You will be dealing with your ability to reject the null hypothesis, which is that there is no real difference between the sample results and the population. *Statistical power* refers to the statistical ability to reject the null hypothesis when it is false, saying that the difference is real. It takes a large sample to reach a satisfactory level of statistical power.

Significance, the level of confidence at which you reject the null hypothesis and say the results are not due to chance, is affected by the size of the effect. It takes a large difference to reach a satisfactory level of statistical significance. However, at a given confidence level, the greater the difference (impact) you expect, the smaller your sample has to be.

Sample size is a statistical issue that should be discussed with a consultant or specialist, taking into consideration your expected results before a final decision is made.

Instrument selection and design deals with validity (Does the test measure what it is supposed to?), reliability (Does the test get consistent results in comparable circumstances?), appropriateness (Is the test fair?), and bias (Does the test systematically give better or worse results for a population for reasons irrelevant to the test purpose?).

It is best to avoid creating brand-new test instruments during the funding period unless that is the original reason for the funding or it is crucial for the evaluation, as in tests of knowledge. To design an instrument just for the evaluation may mean spending time and resources out of proportion to the project's needs. Always check the literature to see whether existing instruments are available. To develop good instruments requires criteria for reliability and validity. The steps are presented in Chapter 12 in the section on practical considerations.

Data as a topic relates to the nature of what is collected. If you collect information or ask questions that result in open-ended responses, yes or no, or rank orders, you will be creating nominal or ordinal variables. Responses that can be placed on graduated scales such as height, weight, or other expressions of graduated quantity create interval or ratio variables.

Analysis has to do with the types of statistical procedures to be applied to the data. The choice of techniques is limited by the form of the data and the available resources. If you know that you will be interested in the relationships among a complex set of variables, you will wish to do parametric and multivariate analysis such as multiple correlation analysis, factor analysis, or cluster analysis. These require that your data come from interval or ratio scales and that the variables be normally distributed in the population. For rank order data or frequency distributions, nonparametric analysis is appropriate, such as paired comparisons, contingency tables, and chi-square distribution.

If you plan to use experimental design, consult experts to help you make the best decisions. For quasi-experimental design, this text or a basic evaluation text offer enough options. A statistics text is useful. The point is to know beforehand what you want to ask and the statistical tests that allow you to generalize with statistical authority. Then you can select those most appropriate for your data and test instruments.

Reports are the way in which evaluation results are disseminated. At the very least you owe the funding agency a final report. Beyond that, you may be offering (as a product) a report that will make a contribution to the literature and may even be publishable. Do not underestimate the possibilities for extending the knowledge in the field, as well as for advancing your career.

QUALITATIVE ANALYSIS

Formative evaluation is relevant for pilot tests, dry runs, feasibility studies, and process evaluation covering milestones and products. Sometimes there may be a need for heavy-duty quantitative statistical analysis, but much of the work calls for qualitative analysis.

Qualitative analysis covers both simple comparisons between promised and actual achievements and sophisticated techniques that bring to bear judgment and subjective analysis for use in the specific project situation. Examples of such techniques are case histories, open-ended interviews, diaries, retrospective accounts by participants, unstructured observation reports, content analysis, and expert judgments.

The major distinction between quantitative and qualitative techniques is that qualitative results cannot be the basis for generalizations, since they are not based on large numbers and do not rely on predetermined objective criteria.

If qualitative techniques are appropriate for some of your objectives, be sure the funder sees how you are avoiding the main dangers: bias, after-the-fact criteria, and inappropriate selection of criteria.

PROJECT MONITORING

Every project proposal should have a section that deals with evaluation of the project's functioning. This can be called *project monitoring* and it is a form of process evaluation or formative evaluation.

Project monitoring answers the question, Is the project being carried out as promised, in a timely way, with the quality and quantities promised? Your monitoring design for the proposal should indicate that you will be assessing the functioning of the project on a regular basis and that any problems will be caught early and corrected.

Having presented due dates for project activities in your plan of work, you would indicate how you will monitor the activities to see that they are successfully reached. You would explain how you will monitor staff performance, client satisfaction, delivery of the program components on time, and other factors that affect the way the method is being delivered. You might describe how you will deal with cost containment on a regular basis. In each case, you would show how the monitoring will make improvements possible.

Client satisfaction can be evaluated using direct questionnaires, using data on appointment keeping, lateness, absence, attendance, complaints, compliance, and rap sessions. *Employee performance* may be rated by observers, through supervisory reports, or by measures of output quality or quantity.

12

Writing the Evaluation Section

INTRODUCTION

This chapter presents guidelines for writing, discusses what should be covered in the evaluation section, and offers a practical schematic layout that will help to organize the section if it is done prior to writing.

The initial ideas for the evaluation design have already been prefigured in the objectives. Now you must translate the ideas into a feasible set of steps, some of which imply the expenditure of time and money solely for design purposes. How elaborate your evaluation should be is a function of the expected resources and of whether rigorous evaluation design is appropriate for your stage in developing the method.

Be sure to discuss your plans for the evaluation design with those in your agency with whom you are cooperating. They can be helpful in guiding you on the limitations you may face in doing an extensive or elaborate evaluation, or any ethical or practical considerations. Agreement on what will be done, coordination of activities, and common standards of competence for the evaluation are important.

Also, note that the funding agency may require specific evaluation techniques. If you are seeking federal funds, check the criteria for selecting proposals in the *Catalog of Federal Domestic Assistance* and/or the funding agency's guidelines. The federal government asks that problems be well defined, that relationships between facts, events, and explanations (theory) be analyzed, and that an evaluation include the collection of data *before* and *during* project operations.

GUIDELINES FOR WRITING

The following is a general outline for the evaluation section.

1. You would generally open with a brief statement about the general purposes of evaluation. You would describe the type of project objectives you have and the appropriate type of evaluation design for the objectives. That is, if your project objectives relate to testing a method, you would discuss the extent to which experimental design applies. But if you were dealing with a planning grant, you would be talking about process evaluation.

2. You would discuss the qualifications of the person to be in charge of the evaluation. It is OK to have a consultant for the design of the evaluation or to supervise the data collection, perform the statistical analysis, and help interpret the results. But the project director must be responsible for knowing what will be done and why, and for the major interpretation and report writing. The qualifications of anyone in charge of evaluation should be impressive and mentioned in the text, while the reader is referred to an appendix to see a resume. The qualifications for process-type evaluation design are less demanding. If you do not have someone on board who will be in charge, describe the qualifications you will require.

3. Each objective or set of grouped objectives should be stated so the reader knows to what you are referring; the success criteria should be identified; the subjects involved, if any, should be described, including numbers, the basis for selection, and their key characteristics; the data to be collected, the instrument, times of collection, and type of data should be given, and by whom collected. There should be a statement of the types of analysis to be done or comparisons to be made.

4. Then you would provide a chronological sequence of evaluation events within the project period. (You may refer the reader to your plan of work, appearing later in the proposal.)

5. You would go on to discuss project monitoring and use of the results to improve the project.

6. You would end with discussion of the final report and dissemination of the results.

Sequencing the Evaluation Section

You would arrange and present your objectives in the order that would make the most sense to the reader. You could present your project objectives in order, from long-range goals to broad objectives, to behavioral objectives, to intermediary objectives, with the process objectives in chronological order of the dates they are due.

You may wish to show how an educational objective will affect the behavioral objectives, which in turn affect the broad objectives, and present the project objectives in that order, but only if that applies to your project.

You could arrange all your objectives in the order that they are due. The main thing you are attempting to do is to repeat each objective and then tell how you will evaluate it.

PRACTICAL CONSIDERATIONS

The secret of evaluation design is imagination. If the project is not real to you, staffed with real people carrying out real activities with real clients, you will be in trouble in the evaluation section, which requires mental visualization. You have to be able to see exactly what will be going on, step by step, to design a practical evaluation.

Evaluation of Project Objectives

When designing the evaluation of project objectives, consider how you will obtain the test (study) group members. Do you want to include everyone who receives the intervention, or a sample? That can depend on the ease with which you can access the participants for pre- and post-testing. Will the measurement-taking be easily integrated into the regular contact with them in the project? Or will there be a major extra effort, especially for posttests? Also consider the amount of staff effort required to administer the tests. Are the measures going to be collected anyway? Are you planning on mail-backs with low response rates, telephone interviews, or face-to-face personal contact?

How many posttests do you need? That depends on the relative importance of measuring attenuation (falling off) or the sleeper effect (improvement) at intervals after the intervention. Will your funding period and design allow several posttests? If the intervention is brief, say several weeks, and if the project starts early in the funding period, with several sequential intervention groups passing through, you can follow the early groups for several posttests. But consider how you will get the subjects to cooperate with the posttesting, since there is no real incentive for them.

Do not do midintervention testing unless you have a special reason. Such testing offers very little information. Sometimes this is mistakenly offered instead of monitoring of the processes involved in delivering the program or service.

Consider whether you can obtain a comparable control or comparison group. Can you ethically assign randomly and withhold treatment from one group? Can you delay treatment for a group while it serves as a control group, and then administer the treatment? Can you go elsewhere for a comparable group? What can you offer to gain cooperation?

Will the control or comparison group be contaminated by contact with the study group? How will you deal with that? Will your controls be available for both pre- and posttesting? Consider the same questions raised above about cooperation for pre- and posttesting.

If your project objectives predict changes in individual characteristics that vary in the study group, such as changes for those who are overweight when not all are overweight, be clear on how you will identify such individuals in the pretest and follow them to the posttest. If you select anonymous self-reporting to increase reliability, how do you keep track? There are solutions; tell about them.

If you rely on self-reporting, how will you assist your subjects to accurately report items that are intimate or based on memory, such as smoking, protected sexual behavior, or diet?

If you have intermediary project objectives such as educational objectives, remember to state among your success criteria your hypothesis that the subjects who do well on the educational objectives, or are more exposed to the educational intervention, will do better on the behavioral and/or broad objectives. To test this you can do correlation analysis among the two sets of measures or do subgroup analysis based on scores on the intermediary criteria.

Evaluation of Process Objectives

When designing the evaluation of process objectives, remember that success criteria are *proofs* of success. So meeting a due date must be evidenced by some act, such as written approval, announcement of something starting, staffing, or some other tangible indicator.

If a process objective is the creation of a test or survey instrument, you should include field tests in your evaluation design and use validity, reliability, and related measures for success criteria. You field test on small, separate, but known groups. You test and revise to attain the following criteria, allowing enough time to test, revise, and retest:

1. The questions must be understandable to those who will be tested.

2. Tests for the need for or effects of training should show that test items are answered correctly by individuals known to be competent and are not answered correctly by untrained individuals.

3. Test takers should produce highly correlated answers when asked to retake the test after a short period of time (test-retest reliability).

4. Test results should correlate highly with another measure of the same content.

5. Several versions of the same question within the test should be highly correlated. (This is a way of creating posttests during field testing. You put in more items for each content area than you need, and closely correlated items can be apportioned to two versions, one of which is used for the posttest.)

6. Any scales should conform to standards for equal-appearing intervals.

If one of the process objectives is staff training, consider what you will do if some trainees score badly on posttesting. Will they be excluded from the project? Retrained? Will you review the curriculum or the trainer? With medical interventions, some absolute standards are needed to safeguard the patients.

SCHEMATIC LAYOUT OF EVALUATION DESIGN

Figure 12.1 is a schematic layout of the basic elements of the evaluation design. Not all of the layout is applicable to all proposals. Select only those parts that apply to *your* objectives.

The schematic layout of the evaluation components is helpful for writing the evaluation design section because it helps you focus and see how the parts interrelate. It is similar to the layout of the basic program components introduced in Chapter 9. It is an outline of your main points, rather than a detailed elaboration. It can help you group objectives to be served by the same design and remind you of the process objectives: products and milestones, and the monitoring that must be included.

After working with the schematic layout, you may wish to rewrite your objectives so that they more precisely incorporate your success criteria and test instruments. You may also notice, after developing your success criteria, that your objectives are worded in a way that is too focused on the benefits to your organization (such as an increase in

FIGURE 12.1

Basic Schematic Evaluation Design Layout

OBJECTIVES	DUE DATES	SUCCESS CRITERION	DESIGN ELEMENTS
Project Objectives: Broad/Main Behavioral	Group those with common design and due dates. Start: "By the end of the __th month...."	Give the change to be achieved "_____, as measured by (give figure and measuring instrument) compared with (give the comparison base, such as pre-test /post-test change compared with a comparison group, etc.)"	Present the selection of controls and test subjects, how moderator variables will be dealt with; data collection, and other details.
Project Objectives: Educational Intermediary	Same as above	Same as above	Same as above
Process Objectives: Products Milestones in chronological order by date due	Same as above	Give the quality or quantity to be reached, how measured or by whom evaluated, credentials of evaluater, standards to be met, or what applies.	Describe any special circumstances, data collection dates, and other details.
Project Monitoring	Dates of monitoring activity	Name the quality/quantity aspects of project functioning to be monitored.	Describe how the monitoring will be done; how feedback will be used.

clients), rather than on the benefits to your clients. If that is the case, go back and refocus the objectives to these latter considerations.

Follow up by developing more emphasis on the methodology to accomplish the target-population oriented outcomes. Without such a refocus you will not get funded, because funding agencies are concerned about benefits to the target populations.

Do not be surprised if, in doing the layout, you discover that you have left out an objective or two. That is what the exercise is for. If this happens, remember to go back and follow up with a problem and a methods statement.

EXAMPLES

Exhibit 12 is an example of a schematic evaluation design layout, and Exhibit 13 presents two examples of evaluation design sections. Notice that the order presented in the layout need not be followed in the proposal.

Also, note that the work done in the layout can be refined in the process of working on the final wording in the proposal, and that both the layout and the section on evaluation may require you to go back to revise the original section on objectives. You may find discrepancies in details if you compare Exhibits 8, 12 and 13. See if you can spot the items, and decide what you would do.

EXHIBIT 12
Example of Schematic Evaluation Design Layout: Education of Parents of Infants Discharged from Intensive Care

Objectives	Due Dates	Success Criterion	Design Elements
Project Objectives			**Quasi-experimental**
1. For test group infants of test group parent(s), 18 months post NICU discharge: rates will be lower than for the comparison group in	End of 35th month	As measured by hospital records; records obtained by follow up inquiries; death records; clinic records	**design,** using pre/post testing; a comparison group of infants based on retrospective data, and no comparison group for the parents. Reason is ethics of withholding an intervention expected to save lives.
a. Mortality		20% lower	**Infant test group**
b. Morbidity		25% lower	First 100 infants who
c. Developmental delays		25% lower	qualify whose parents complete the program and agree to testing will be
2. The test group parents of test group infants, 18 months post NICU discharge will	End of 35th month	As measured by clinic records	followed for 18 months. **Comparison group** 100 infants discharged 18 months before the 1st day of program, counting back to obtain 100 for
a. be in compliance with recommended schedule of clinic visits.		90% of test group; 90% compliance	whom there are 18 mos. medical records post-discharge, including any deceased during 18 mos.
b. demonstrate appropriate behavior in	End of 17th month	As measured by simulation tests of life situations	For demonstration study sample is large enough to replace need for random assignment/match
i. parenting (nurturing, stimulation, exercise, infection control)		Scores of 85% or better for 85% of group	pairs. Effect of time difference not known.
ii. response to emergencies		Pre-test scores below 70% will rise to 75% or better	**Parent test group** From 100 to 200 parents of eligible infants who agree to participate in study.
iii. monitoring of developmental delays		Definitions	Moderator variables on which data will be collected on infants:
		Mortality rate Number of infant deaths per hundred discharged from NICU over an 18-month period following discharge. (This rate requires each infant to be followed for 18 months, so that the period for 100 infants could be as long as 28 months, assuming 10 infants per month dis-	weight at birth; diagnosis on arrival in NICU; diagnosis of risk on release; chronic conditions; length of time in NICU; age at release, severity score; race/ethnicity; no. of caregivers in program; other siblings. Parental moderator variables: age; sex; relation to

continued

Objectives	Due Dates	Success Criterion	Design Elements
		charged and qualified. For comparison group the period extends in time from infants whose 18 months end at start of program, backwards until 100 are identified.)	infant; years of education; income; first language; home condition score; number of caregivers in home.
		Morbidity rate Readmission to hospital for medical reason, rate calculated as above	Pretests of behavioral contents will be part of the first training session prior to its start; posttests will be administered as part of the last group session.
		Developmental delay rate Diagnosed developmental delay in cases not medically expected to have such delay, rate calculated as above	Pretests of knowledge contents will be part of the first training session, after the behavioral component. Posttests will be part of the last training session, at the end.
3. Test group parents of test group infants 18 months post NICU discharge will show mastery of subject matter covered in training	End of 17th month	As measured by paper-and-pencil tests of relevant knowledge and information.	
a. parenting (nurturing, stimulation, exercise, infection control)		Scores of 85% or better for 85% of group Pre-test scores below 70% rise to 75% or better	
b. response to emergencies			
c. monitoring of developmental delays			
d. need for clinic follow-up care			
4. Test group parents of test group infants 18 months post NICU discharge will demonstrate that training affects behavior and infant mortality and morbidity rates.	End of 35th month	As measured by multivariate analysis of infant scores on mortality, morbidity and developmental delays, parent scores on behavior/knowledge tests and moderator variables Inverse, significant correlation between infant scores and parent behavioral scores; and direct, significant correlation between parent behavioral scores including completion rate, and parent knowledge scores	

continued

EXHIBIT 12, continued

Objectives	Due Dates	Success Criterion	Design Elements
Process Objectives:			
5. Curriculum content selection in final form.	End of 1st month	Approval from 2 senior staff and 2 faculty consultants in written form	
6. Video tapes for training ready for use in English Spanish French Korean(?)	End of 4th month	Approval from 2 senior staff, 2 faculty, 4 parent representatives in written form	
7. Handout for use at home giving home care guide-lines, ready for use in above languages	End of 4th month	Approval from 2 senior staff, 2 faculty, 4 parent representatives in written form	
8. Six NICU nurse educators, inclu-ding one from each of 3 cooper-ating hospitals, trained and ready to lead the discussion groups	End of 6th month	Approved after observa-tion in a dry run with representatives of the parent population, by one of 2 senior staff or 2 faculty consultants, on observation forms	Parent participants in review committees, dry runs of training components, preparation of the video tapes, and field testing of the pre/post tests will be individuals with infants in NICU care, prior to the start of the project, selected to reflect language and educational levels in the target population, with emphasis on lower educational attainment and ethnic/racial diversity.
9. Outreach material describing train-ing ready for use	End of 6th month	Approval by 2 senior staff and 2 represen-tatives of parents, by signature	
10. Procedures for referral to parent training and clinic ser-vices in place	End of 6th month	Memorandum on procedures in standard operations manual, and staff memo acknowledged by all staff involved, including supervisors, at all four hospitals for clinic referrals	
11. Record forms for use in recording referrals, health status, moderator variables, atten-dance, observa-tions, etc., in place	End of 6th month	Approval by director of project and evaluation specialist; use checked by site visits	
12. Clinic services on stream	End of 7th month	Staff assigned and in attendance as indicated by site visits	
13. Training program on stream	End of 7th month	Parents attending video presentations and dis-cussion groups as indi-cated by site visits	
14. Pre/post video tests for use in evaluation of	End of 7th month	Successful completion of field tests to determine that test items meet the	Test construction and field testing will draw on "naive" parents not

continued

Objectives	Due Dates	Success Criterion	Design Elements
behavioral objectives (simulation tests); response sheets and observation formats ready for use Paper and pencil tests for knowledge and information ready for use		following criteria: the test items will be comprehensible to a representative sample. Test items will be answered correctly by at least 80 percent of the population sample known to be "experts" in the content; Test items will be answered incorrectly by at least 80 percent of the population sample known to be "ignorant" about content. Multiple versions of the same items should correlate at .9 or better. Test/retest scores should correlate at .9 or better	involved in the preparation of the training material who are interviewed to determine true "ignorance" of training content, and trained parents and staff who are interviewed to determine true "expert" status. Field test groups will include five in each category, and draw on others for further testing after revision.
15. Preliminary training tapes and program materials available for use by others	End of 30th month	Arrangement to copy tapes in place; Persons on mailing list informed.	
16. Parents of infants eligible to be in program will be participating	End of 35th month	As measured by: referral and attendance records. 95%+ of eligible infants with 1 or more parents participating.	Attendance will be taken at group sessions and sign up sheets will track parents' use, completion and reuse of videos at the main hospital and clinic satellites.
17. Participating parents completing training	End of 35th month	As measured by pre/post test scores and attendance records. 80%+ of participants attending 80%+ of time.	
18. Results of evaluation available for distribution	End of 36th month	Persons on mailing list informed.	
19. Revised training tapes and program materials available for distribution	End of 36th month		
Project Monitoring Staff functioning, parents' participation and satisfaction will be monitored by spot checks and interviews every two months to catch problems as they develop.	Bi-monthly	Positive responses from participants; Good evaluations of functioning.	Monitoring results will be used to make any needed adjustments in the delivery of the program.
Project deadlines will be compared with work progress to be sure project is on target.	Weekly	Work activities on schedule; mini evaluation checks to note any unanticipated problems.	

EXHIBIT 13
Examples of Evaluation Sections

Example 1: Education for Parents of Infants Discharged from Intensive Care

EVALUATION

Evaluation will be an integral part of the project and is designed to determine the success of the program as well as to monitor ongoing project operations. The evaluation design is the result of the collaboration of Dr. ____, who will be the project director, and Dr. ____, who has been responsible for evaluation design in several other projects funded at the hospital.

Two staff members with masters-level training, drawn from the medical records department, will be added to the project during periods of data collection, including the collection of retrospective information for a comparison group and follow-up data on test-group members. (See Appendix __ for staff vitae.)

The presentation of the evaluation design here is in chronological order of the due dates for objectives, and the numbers do not correspond with those in the section on objectives.

Process Objectives

Process objectives are the activities and products needed to make the project objectives possible. Each will be evaluated as follows:

1. Selection of curriculum content will be completed by the end of the first month. The success criterion is written approval by a committee of senior staff, including a patient educator, a NICU nurse, the director, and faculty consultants from ____ College.

2. Video training tapes (10 two-hour tapes in English, Spanish, French, and perhaps Korean) and a handout in each language, for use at home, giving guidelines for infant care, will be ready for use by the end of the 4th month. The success criterion is approval by a committee of two senior staff members, two faculty members, and four representatives of the parent target population.

Note: Parent participants in review committees, dry runs of training components, preparation of video tapes, and field testing of the pre- and posttests will be individuals with infants in NICU care prior to the start of the parent training, selected to reflect the languages and educational levels of the target population, with emphasis on those with least educational attainment and ethnic/racial diversity, to ensure that the material will be appropriate to the audience for which it is designed.

By the end of the sixth month,

3. Six nurse educators, including one from each of the three cooperating hospitals, who will work in the clinics, will be trained and ready to lead discussion groups as part of the training program. The success criterion is approval on observation forms created for the purpose, by a team of staff and faculty observers in a dry-run presentation with parent groups.

4. Outreach material describing the training and indicating the necessity of the training prior to discharge from the NICU will be ready for use. The success criterion is approval by the review committee.

continued

5. Institutional procedures for referring parents to training and to clinic services will be in place. The success criteria are as follows: a memorandum on procedures for referral will be in the standard procedures book; the staff will have attended a meeting about them; and the procedure will be acknowledged by all the relevant supervisors. The clinic procedures will also be incorporated into the work practice of the staffs at the three cooperating clinic sites.

6. Record forms will be in place for use in case histories and charting, to be used for the evaluation design, for referrals, for attendance at video and group sessions, and for observation of staff functioning. The success criteria are approval by Drs. ____ and ____ and spot checks at sites during the eighth month to make sure they are being used properly.

By the end of the seventh month,

7. The training program will be operational; the clinic services will be available. The success criteria are staff assignments made and attendance by parents.

8. Pre- and post-test versions for the behavioral contents, using videotaped simulations, response sheets, and observational testing for CPR, will be ready for use; paper-and-pencil tests and response sheets for the knowledge-content pre- and post-tests will be ready for use. The success criteria are field test results indicating that the test items are comprehensible to individuals similar to the target population; that the items are answered correctly by at least 80 percent of the sample population independently verified as "experts" and answered incorrectly by at least 80 percent of the sample population independently verified as "not competent" in the content; that multiple versions of the same items correlate at .9 or better; and that test-retest scores correlate at .9 or better.

Test construction and field testing will draw on "naive" parents not involved in preparation of the training materials or pilot training. The "experts" will be parents who received pilot training and staff members. There will be five members in each field-test group; assignment to a group by knowledge level will be independently verified by interview.

Project Objectives

By the end of the 17th month,

9. Test-group parents of test-group infants will demonstrate mastery of required knowledge presented in the training on paper-and-pencil tests in the following areas:

a. Parenting, including nurturing, stimulation, exercise, and infection control.
b. Recognition of emergencies such as cardiopulmonary distress and knowledge of what to do.
c. Monitoring of developmental delays.
d. Understanding of the need for clinic follow-up care.

continued

The success criteria are that, of the test group, 85 percent will show scores of 85 percent or better on posttests, and those with pretest scores below 70 percent will show rises to 75 percent or better on posttests.

Note: No comparison group will be used, because withholding the intervention involves possible effects on mortality and morbidity. The parent test group will be studied in small sequential groups over a long period, so any effects of trend will be noticeable. The parent test group will include from 100 to 200 caregivers (one or two to an eligible infant) of infants expected to be discharged from the NICU and eligible for the project, who agree to be studied.

Moderator variables for learning and behavioral outcomes for which data will be collected are age, sex, relation to infant, years of education, income, first language, home condition score (reflecting the quality and safety of the home and stability of the family), and number of caregivers at home. Pretests of knowledge will be part of the first training session, after the behavioral component is tested. Posttests will be part of the last training session, after it ends.

10. Test-group parents of test-group infants will demonstrate mastery of required behaviors presented in simulation tests presenting life situations in the following areas:

a. Parenting, including nurturing, stimulation, exercise, and infection control.
b. Proper response to emergencies such as cardiopulmonary distress and demonstration of what to do.
c. Monitoring of developmental delays.

The success criteria are that 85 percent will show scores of 85 percent or better on posttests, and those with pretest scores below 70 percent will show rises to 75 percent or better on posttests.

Pretests of behavior will be part of the first training session, prior to its start, and posttests will be administered after the last group session.

By the end of the 35th month,

11. Test-group parents of test-group infants will be in compliance with the recommended schedule of clinic visits, as measured by clinic records. The success criteria are that 90 percent will be in compliance with 90 percent or better of the scheduled or recommended visits.

12. Test-group infants of test-group parents, 18 months after discharge from the NICU, will show lower rates of mortality, morbidity, and developmental delays than a comparison group, as measured by hospital records, records obtained through follow-up inquiries, death records, and clinic records. The success criteria are that mortality will be 20 percent lower and morbidity and developmental delays will be 25 percent lower than in the comparison group.

The infant test group will include the first 100 infants who qualify to be in the program whose parents agree to participate in the study. The comparison group will

continued

include 100 infants discharged 18 months or more before the first day of the program, counting back to obtain 100 infants for whom there are records for the 18 months since their discharge, including deceased infants who die prior to the 18 months. This size sample substitutes for the advantages of random selection; however, the effects of time will be unknown, except for regional trends in public data for comparison purposes.

Moderator variables for which data will be collected for the infant test group will include weight at birth, sex, race/ethnicity, diagnosis/prognosis upon arrival at NICU, diagnosis/prognosis upon discharge, presence of chronic conditions, length of time in NICU, age at release, severity of condition at release, number of caregivers participating in the program, number of other siblings, number of caregivers in the home, the condition-of-home score, and other parental variables.

Definitions

Mortality rate for purposes of the study: number of infant deaths in 18 months post-NICU discharge per 100 discharged. (This rate is based on the 18-month period after an infant's discharge; it is not the rate for a given calendar period.)

Morbidity rate for purposes of the study: the number of readmissions to a hospital for medical reasons, with the rate calculated as above.

Developmental delay rate for purposes of the study: number of diagnosed developmental delays not expected from the medical condition of the infant upon discharge, with the rate calculated as above.

13. The infants with parents in the program will show mortality, morbidity, and developmental delay rates that correlate significantly and inversely with parent scores on the behavioral posttests; their parents' scores on the behavioral-posttest will correlate significantly and directly with scores on educational posttests, as measured by multivariate and subgroup analysis, taking moderator variables into account.

Process Objectives

By the end of the project period,

14. Participation of parents in the program as measured by referral and attendance records at video screening locations and group sessions will meet the success criteria; that 95 percent of eligible infants will have one or two participants attending training, and 80 percent of the participants will complete the training.

15. The results of the evaluation and revised copies of the training materials will be available for distribution. The success criteria are that arrangements will have been made to copy the tapes for distribution, and persons on the mailing list compiled for distribution purposes will be informed of their availability.

Example 4: Writing Skills for Retention of Graduate Students

EVALUATION

The project design includes evaluation design to determine how well the project objectives were accomplished and to provide for regular monitoring of project activity.

continued

The evaluation will be under the direction of the director, Professor ____, who is also director of the masters program in ____. Dr. ____ has had experience in research design and is responsible for evaluation of student research in her graduate program.

The evaluation design is primarily focused on attainment of levels of student and faculty functioning and, as a start-up demonstration project, is not an attempt at program trial, which would call for experimental design. However, the design calls for rigorous adherence to success criteria. Below are the objectives to be met, their dates for completion, and the criteria that will be applied to measure success.

Project and Process Objectives

By the end of the third year,

1. Of the candidates for admission to the cooperating graduate programs who are rejected for deficient writing skills, 80 percent will be accepted after one or two semesters' enrollment in the basic writing course. This will be measured by records of application decisions, enrollment in the courses, and attendance at the writing tutorials.

2. Of the matriculated students in danger of having grade-point averages below 3.0 who attend the writing tutorials and/or the basic writing course, 80 percent will be maintaining above 3.0 averages, as measured by records of faculty referrals, attendance at tutorials, enrollment, and grade records.

3. Of the students responding who complete the basic and intermediate writing courses and/or attend the writing tutorials, 80 percent will express the opinion that the writing help has been effective, measured by their own sense of accomplishment.

4. Of the students in the basic writing class, 90 percent will reach the goals set at the start of the semester in conference with the instructor.

5. Of the students taking the basic or intermediate classes in writing and/or the writing tutorials, 95 percent or more will show pretest-posttest improvement in scores.

6. Admissions testing for writing skills and referral will be routine, as indicated by records of referrals and use of tests.

7. The faculty will be grading for writing skills and will be referring students to classes and/or tutorials, as indicated by referral data.

8. Graduate advisors will be evaluating students with low grades and, if warranted, will refer them to writing classes and/or tutorials, as indicated by records and attendance.

9. The president of the college will be seeking a permanent line to continue the work in graduate remediation.

Process Objectives

By the end of the second year,

10. An award for graduate writing will be a regular part of graduation recognition.

11. Enrollments in two basic writing courses per year and one intermediate writing course per year will reach the class maximum of 15–16 students each semester.

continued

12. Approximately 40 students, averaging four one-hour sessions per semester, will be attending the writing tutorials on school premises, and 50 percent will come from faculty referrals.

13. The college senate will have approved the two writing courses.

Process Objectives

By the end of the first project year,

14. A graduate writing test will be available that can be answered on one page, take no more than 20 minutes, be graded in five minutes using a standard guide, and will be in use by admissions officers and graduate advisors. Criteria will include interrater reliability of .85 and the ability to discriminate those needing basic remediation from those needing more advanced help.

15. The faculty will have participated in meetings to promote the use of writing standards in grading and will know how to make referrals to the three types of writing assistance.

16. The dean of the school will ask the faculty to include writing in grading standards and to make referrals.

17. Evaluation forms will be field tested and ready for use.

18. Data record forms for evaluation will be designed and in use.

19. Classes will be on stream; the equivalent of one full-time faculty member will be teaching two courses in the fall and one in the spring and will be offering writing tutorial help from 4 to 8 P.M. in the remaining time.

Dissemination of Results

The results of the evaluation design will be presented in a report to the funding agency and to the college community, encouraging application in other programs and colleges. The faculty members involved will be available as consultants to help, and the writing test will be offered for publication.

Project Monitoring

Project activities will be monitored for adherence to projected due dates. Ongoing attention to schedules will help ensure timely attainment of project objectives. Snags in the execution of the program will be caught early and corrected and the work allowed to continue. The faculty is routinely evaluated by peers and students; these evaluations will be included as part of the overall attention to quality.

13

Plan of Work

When you have completed your evaluation design, you have all the information needed to lay out a plan of work. This becomes the basis for providing effective project monitoring, is a framework for deciding on staffing patterns, and helps in developing a budget. It will also show up any gaps in your planning and timing.

The basic design requires a listing of all the activities in which you will engage in carrying out the project, from the early start-up tasks to the last phasing out. These are arranged so that it is clear what activities will be going on in any given month.

The funding agency's proposal guidelines may ask for a plan of work, a section on level of effort, or a time line. These are all similar. If something of this sort is not called for, you should provide it anyway. A good plan of work shows the funding agency that you have a clear idea of what you will be doing and enhances your credibility. The section can be placed after the evaluation section, as in this book, or can come just before the budget section. In a preapplication it can be an appendix.

The plan of work is introduced by a brief narrative telling about the activities and resources needed. It then generally provides a chart or table with details.

OPTIONAL FORMATS

The simplest design for a plan of work lists the main activities of the project in a column in the order that they first appear and arrays the months of the project as column headings to the right, as seen in Section A of Figure 13.1. Then a checkmark is placed under each month that the activity will occur. Remember to include the activities required to produce

FIGURE 13.1
Examples of Plan-of-Work Layouts

Section A

ACTIVITY (e.g.) MONTH:	1	2	3	4	5	6	7	8	9	10	11	12
Outreach	E		X	X	X							
	X											
Evaluation	A			X		X				X	X	X
	M											
Program	P			X	X	X	X	X	X	X	X	
	L											
Phase-out	E										X	X

Section B

PERIOD	ACTIVITY	STAFF AND FACILITIES
Month 1	Staffing Design of informational packet Selection of subjects Design of announcements	Project Director Patient Educator Support staff Duplicating equipment

Section C

Milestone	Milestone or Criterion Activity	Month

6. Evaluation
    Design
4. Design
    Curriculum
 	
3. Outreach
	Engage support staff
	Design evaluation instruments
	Engage instructor
	Arrange for reviewer
	Order materials
	Design announcement letter to potential subjects
	Get mailing list from central office
		First
		Month

Section D

Month 1 Month 2 Month 3 Month 4 Month 5 Month 6 Month 7 Month 8 Month 9 Month 10

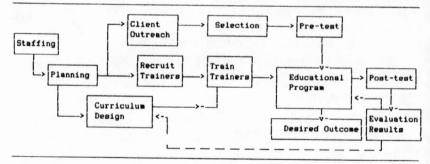

140

the process objectives, your products and milestones, and the work involved in evaluation, such as collection of baseline data, selection of subjects, and pre- and posttesting. Remember to allow for project monitoring, report writing, and contingencies. Note that the Figure 13.1 illustrations are abbreviated; actual plans would have many more items.

Another approach is illustrated in Section B of the figure. This presents a table in which the chronological due dates are listed in a column and the milestone activities in the adjacent column. Next to that the required staff and facilities are listed. This is appropriate when the funding agency asks for a section on level of effort.

A more elaborate presentation of your plan of work is illustrated in Section C of the figure. This presents the steps needed to achieve the objectives as a numbered set of milestones, including success criteria presented in the evaluation section. The right-hand column presents the months. The left-hand column presents the milestone number and a descriptive phrase. The center column lists the activity planned for that month to achieve the milestone. The months appear in chronological order, and each activity is presented for every month in which it will be worked on. You can set dates earlier in this layout than the promised due dates and thus build in contingency planning.

A sophisticated fourth approach is Project Evaluation and Review Technique (PERT). Section D shows a schematic representation of a PERT plan. It shows how each step feeds into other steps at critical dates. You begin with objectives promised on specific due dates and work back through the prior steps. This allows you to supervise the work flow and, if there are delays, pick up at once on the consequences.

It is important to list the work separately for each year, because projects are funded from year to year, and you should be able to show visually what will be delivered in any given year. Examples of plans of work are presented in Exhibit 14.

EXHIBIT 14
Examples of Plan-of-Work Sections

PLAN OF WORK

The proposed organization of activity for the project is represented in Table 2,
which presents our plan of work. It shows each activity in the order it first
occurs, with an x mark in every month it takes place.

Table _. Plan of Work For Women of Color Leadership Project: One Project Year

Activity Month:	1	2	3	4	5	6	7	8	9	10	11	12
1 Create advisory board	x											
2 Announce project	x											
3 Identify women of color in states	x	x	x	x								
4 Develop format for collecting recommendations	x											
5 Project staff meetings	x	x	x	x	x	x	x	x	x	x	x	x
6 Distribute format		x	x	x	x	x	x	x	x	x	x	x
7 Task force recommendations			x	x	x	x	x	x	x	x	x	x
8 Integrate recommendations into Project-distributed information			x	x	x	x	x	x	x	x	x	
9 Quarterly and annual reports			x	x		x				x		x
10 Distribute recommendations to states				x	x	x	x	x	x	x	x	x
11 Provide technical assistance				x	x	x	x	x	x	x	x	x
12 Evaluate task forces etc.										x	x	x	x

Example 4: Writing Skills for Retention of Graduate Students

LEVEL OF EFFORT

The guidelines provided by the Office of Education show an April 1 starting date,
so the time line presented in the material below assumes that starting date. We
also show the period of academic inactivity; in the case of ____ College, students
finish classes in mid December and late May. The months of June, July, August, and
January are times when only the faculty may be found on campus. The work has been
planned accordingly, with minimal costs in the summer months and in January.
(Faculty members who work in the June-August period are entitled to extra pay.)

Staffing for the project includes a project director at 25 percent release time; an
administrative director; the associate dean, at 15 percent release time (a grantee
contribution); one faculty line divided between a specialist in teaching writing to
adults, especially English as a second language; a professional writer trained in
journalism and with experience in the field of health and social service, who also
has taught writing; and one part-time graduate student assistant to help collect
data and serve as an advisor. Other faculty participation will be voluntary; no
additional support personnel are needed.

continued

Facilities needed are minimal, requiring only funds for duplication of materials, furnishing a writing workshop office on the School's campus, and the purchase of statistical package software for the personal computer in the director's office for the evaluation work. Project needs are presented in Table _, below.

Table _. Projected Schedule, Staff, and Resource Needs, First Project Year, Graduate Writing Project, April 1, 1989 to March 31, 1990

Date	Activity	Staff/Facilities
April May	Coordination of project activities with participating academic programs planned or begun Preparation of writing workshop schedule/approval Final design of two course outlines and reading lists Development/approval of data forms Design and field testing of simple evaluation forms Schedule for faculty meetings approved Faculty meeting on writing standards/referrals Administrative memorandum on writing standards/referrals drafted/approved/distributed Develop writing test for use in screening and as pre- and post-tests Staffing for writing workshop/writing courses done Announce workshops to students/faculty Writing workshop on stream Schedule two writing classes for fall semester Pre-registration for the writing courses. Collect baseline data from programs Select software program and order	Project director Administrative dir. Graduate assistant 5 hours per week Writing faculty for 4 weeks at 3/4 time Workshop furniture/ files Software program
June	Develop writing test for use in screening and as pre- post-tests/field test	Project director: 2 weeks Graduate assistant 5 hours
July, August: No project activity, except registration for classes.		
Sept. Oct. Nov.	Two writing classes and workshop on stream Coordination with other programs Writing pre-test for students before class or workshop Faculty meeting on writing standards/referrals Writing test field tested for inter-rater reliability/revised Schedule spring class Use test in admissions interviews and pre-registration Collect baseline data	Project director Administrative dir. Writing fac. full time Graduate student 3 hours per week
Dec.	Writing post-test for students last day of class/ or workshop	

continued

EXHIBIT 14, continued

Example 1: Education for Parents of Infants Discharged from Intensive Care

PLAN OF WORK
Table _ presents the steps needed to achieve the objectives laid out in the
evaluation section, including the success criteria. The left-hand column presents
the number of the objective and a phrase describing what it is. The center column
shows the activity or milestone achieved. The column on the right presents the
month in which the activity is to be carried out. Some activity dates fall earlier
than the criterion due date to allow for contingencies and flexibility. The
activities are presented in order by number, but only if an activity falls within
plans for a given month. The months are given by their order within the project,
not by calendar names. There is a separate section for each project year.

Table 3. Plan of Work, NICU Parent Education Project: First Year

Project Objective or Criterion	Activity or Milestone	Month
1. Curriculum	Organize review committees. Obtain final approval of curriculum content.	1
2. Video Tapes and Handouts	Organize for videotaping and preparation of handouts. Prepare scripts for videos.	
7. Training	Arrange for installation of viewing equipment at all locations where they will be used. Arrange for rooms for group sessions. Make final selection of staff for training and clinics. Arrange for clinic operations.	
12. Comparison Group	Select comparison group infants based on records. Collect data on criteria and moderator variables from hospital records.	
2. Video Tapes and Handouts	Prepare handouts. Tape videos.	2
6. Data Forms	Design forms for use in project/service delivery.	
7. Training	Arrange for installation of viewing equipment at all locations where they will be used. Arrange for rooms for group sessions. Arrange for clinic operations.	
12. Comparison Group	Select comparison-group infants based on records. Collect data on criteria and moderator variables from hospital records.	
13. Dissemination of Results	Develop mailing list from NICU directories, contacts, and funding agency.	

144

14

Sponsorship/Organizational Capability

FOCUS ON THE GRANTEE

Once the funding agency is interested in the project idea, the next most important question it asks is, Can the grantee carry out the work? Every set of guidelines will have a section in which you are asked to show the capability of the organization in connection with the project idea. Below are some examples of how guideline sections are worded.

Foundation Request for Statement

A statement of the qualifications or capabilities of the organization to carry out the proposed project.

Names, qualifications and experience of persons who will be primarily responsible for implementation of the program. If they have other duties as well, spell out the approximate portion of their time committed to this project. Show why your organization is the logical one to carry out the project. You may wish to provide a brief background sketch on your agency.

Federal Request for Statement

Evidence of the level of expertise of staff of the organization in conducting related research, demonstration, evaluation, training, technical assistance or technology transfer . . . is provided. The applicant provides brief resumes (two pages each) indicating the qualifications of key staff (or position descriptions for anticipated key personnel) and identifies how these qualifications would enable those people to perform their assigned tasks in a project in a competent manner. Evidence that the applicant organization has adequate facilities and resources to carry out a project, and provides evidence in a (three pages or less) corporate capability statement.

These examples give you an idea of how important it is to be convincing about the ability of your agency to do the work. Lists of reasons for project rejection for funding usually include the inadequacy of the statement on organizational capability. Note, it is the statement that is usually at fault, not necessarily the agency's capability.

When you write this section, the point is to prove the case. This is done by establishing your agency's track record in similar or related projects, by presenting the outstanding qualifications of your proposed staff, by describing superior facilities, and/or by describing a unique key relationship of trust, influence, or service in relation to the target population.

WRITING THE SECTION ON ORGANIZATIONAL CAPABILITY

The following can be used as an outline to make sure that you have touched all the bases:

1. Does your agency have competence and expertise in the field? In similar or related programs? Describe the organization's goals, philosophy, and track record in relevant projects with this or other grantors. Document this by describing your past successes, and put back-up material in an appendix.

2. Are expert staff members or consultants to be assigned to the project? Describe the qualifications of key staff members in the text and refer the reader to an appendix containing their resumes. If any positions are open, describe the requirements. If you have illustrious board members or consultants whose expertise is related, include them in the same way.

3. Is the agency in a special relationship with the target population that could ensure the success of the project? For example, a successful sex education program popular with local youth is a good predictor for a drug abuse or suicide prevention program, especially if you have letters to show support and data to prove past success. Describe this and put the letters in an appendix.

4. Does your agency offer special resources in location, facilities, or equipment? For example, being near a park for a day-care center; having an unused ward for a hospice plan; having performance space for an arts project; having a curriculum that works in a closely related field for an educational program. Describe the strengths and refer the reader to back-up material in an appendix.

5. Has the agency demonstrated fiscal and managerial responsibility in the past? Name the grants successfully completed, the degree of success. If not required on separate forms, briefly discuss the agency's plans for compliance in terms of the following (as relevant):

Fiscal reporting procedures to be adopted

Willingness to supply facilities and support to the project

Assurance of compliance with the Civil Rights Act of 1964

Affirmative action plans

Protection of human subjects and informed consent

Organizing this section will mean getting access to institutional information that you may not have at your fingertips. The institution's history of past successes, its mission statement, as well as resumes and letters from the target population, are all materials that get buried in files. You need help for this section.

Meet with people in your agency to design a plan to obtain the materials needed to support the section on organizational capability. Identify each document needed and each person to be contacted. Make sure that the right person is assigned to collect each item. Set due dates; set up a master file. Stay on top of the collection process; do a follow-up. Exhibit 15 presents an example of a section on organizational capability.

EXHIBIT 15
Example of Section on Organizational Capability

Example 4: Writing Skills for Retention of Graduate Students

ORGANIZATIONAL CAPABILITY

The College

_____ College is in a unique position to carry out the proposed project. We are housed in _____ City, a major urban center with a vast minority and poverty population that is drawn to the health and human services areas for jobs. The undergraduate

continued

enrollment of ____ thousand includes 75 percent working students, and 40 percent minority students. Twenty percent of our students are in professional programs, and 50 percent of undergraduate students receive some form of remediation before graduating.

Our Writing Center serves ____ undergraduate students a semester, and was first started with funds awarded by the ____ Foundation. See Appendix __ for a copy of the final report of that project. The undergraduate remediation courses in writing are now fully subscribed, with a one-year waiting list for enrollment.

Faculty

Dr. ____, who will be the project director, has done pioneering work in task analysis and curriculum development for professional education, for which she received 10 years of funding from the U.S. Department of Labor and Department of Health and Human Services. Her work has been applied nationally and abroad.

She also was responsible for the design of the ____ College master's-level Health and Human Services Administration program, which she now directs. This is the program that will house the writing courses. Dr. ____ was responsible for introducing a writing screening test for applicants to her program, which has proven reliable in predicting which candidates will have difficulty carrying out graduate-level work. Her extensive work in research design and evaluation makes her well suited for the work of director, which will be carried out on a 25 percent release-time basis.

Dr. ____, the administrative director, is Associate Dean of the School of Health and Human Services and will be the liaison among the cooperating programs, the Writing Center and the school administration. She has had extensive experience in the education of graduate students of Hispanic background and is responsible for all experimental programs in the school. She will be assigned on a 15 percent release-time basis, as a grantee contribution.

The English department, which runs the remediation programs and the Writing Center, is fortunate to have the expertise of tenured staff members devoted to the academic education of our city's youth.

Professor ____ has written a definitive work on teaching English as a second language and was a consultant in the preparation of the curricula for the two classes presented in Appendix __. She will be a volunteer consultant for the graduate writing tutorials, writing courses, and faculty workshops.

Ms. ____, who is the editor of ____, a professional journal in the human services field, combines training in journalism with a 10-year history of editing and teaching writing to adults. She was the director of the Executive Writing Program sponsored by the U.S. Department of Commerce in the 1970s. This project provided technical support to minority businesses by teaching minority executives to write the documents needed to function efficiently as heads of businesses. Having taught as part of the adjunct faculty at ____ College, Ms. ____ will now be functioning in a full-time capacity. She will be covering three writing courses a year and writing tutorials from 4 to 8 P.M. four days a week, plus two faculty workshops per semester with the support of Professor ____.

continued

Resumes of senior staff and consultants appear in Appendix __, along with the teaching evaluations for the past four years of Professors ____, ____, and ____.

Facilities

The School of Health and Human Services, a satellite campus of ____ College, is house at ____, in a location that places it in the heart of the area where the city's health and human services provider organizations are located. Many of the staffs of the nearby institutions come to study at the school in the evening. Food service, graduate advising, a library, dormitory facilities, and a writing center staffed by graduate students are available at this site.

Administration

As the second-largest public-supported institution of higher education in the city, ____ College has had major experience as a recipient of federal and foundation funds and is in compliance with the required reporting, accounting, and administrative procedures. Administration of grant monies is handled by a central professional staff, and fiscal guidance is available to all grant directors.

15

Support and Endorsement

SUPPORT

Projects that are supported by their intended beneficiaries are more fundable than those that are designed in the absence of such interest. Projects that are attractive to funding agencies are supported by local communities that expect to benefit from their operation, projects supported by specialists in a field who expect the state of the art to be moved forward by the project, and projects that have already been endorsed by the institutions whose cooperation is needed. The reasoning is that the chances for successful results are greater if prior support is evident.

Similarly, when the target population has had a chance to make inputs to the project design or aspects of project functioning, its commitment is likely to be greater, and this, too, makes a project more attractive to a funding agency.

GETTING SUPPORT AND ENDORSEMENT

The first place to look for support is your own agency: the sponsor. It is not enough to have the chief executive officer sign off on the project proposal. A letter indicating the enthusiasm with which your institution is preparing to support the undertaking once it is approved is important. If your administrator can indicate in a letter the probable incorporation of the program after a successful demonstration, that is best.

To make sure that you will get such letters of support, consider getting your agency's chief administrator or board to review and give approval early in the process of grant writing. Plan to involve other vital parties, such as department chiefs, personnel officers, and others needed for the implementation of the project. They will then have a basis for giving approval and writing letters of support.

Significant outside support can come from anyone who will benefit from the project. For example, a community school board can support an arts project for students; parents can support a teenage smoking cessation program; professionals may see a possible contribution to the literature of the discipline; a county medical board can endorse administration of streptokinase in the field by paramedicals; a noted educator may see the need for graduate-level writing remediation. Local government officials who see the public benefit may endorse a program to provide after-school recreation facilities for youth.

Support from the agencies from which cooperation is needed may include, in the community arts project, a letter from the president of the board of education indicating that the schools will cooperate by busing the students to the locations in the arts neighborhood. In the NICU parent-training project, letters of commitment from the three satellite hospitals that will provide clinic services should be presented, and letters from parents interested in helping. In the streptokinase study, a letter from the trade union representing the paramedics, approving the new job activity and the training, would be outstanding, since it would indicate that a major potential problem had been averted.

Evidence of the willingness of other institutions to adopt the program if it is successful is very attractive. For example, other hospitals may be willing to say that they will have paramedics trained to administer streptokinase after it is demonstrated to be effective; the board of education may say it is willing to incorporate trips to the arts community into its curriculum if the demonstration is successful.

From whom the letters of support and endorsement should come is a function of the nature of your project and the actual support you can attract. If at the start of your project planning you met with potential clientele, academics, professionals, politicians, and/or lay persons or groups asking for suggestions and feedback, perhaps using the discussion paper mentioned earlier, these groups and individuals may now be willing to support the proposal in writing.

WRITING THE SECTION ON
SUPPORT AND ENDORSEMENT

The support and endorsement you have obtained is reported in a section of the project proposal. Generally, you would describe the support, quote from letters addressed to the project or institution by the endorser, and send the reader to an appendix to see the actual letter. Letters in appendixes without reference in the text are never read.

Support letters should be addressed to your agency so you can read them, quote from them in the text, and then place the originals in the appendix. Never feel obligated to include a lukewarm letter.

Early involvement with the target population in the planning should also be described in the section on support, if not covered under the methods section.

To organize the work on this section, meet with people in your agency to design a plan to obtain letters of support. It is not always easy to get people to commit to something in writing, and it is sometimes hard to get them to write clearly or with adequate enthusiasm. Sometimes you are asked to send a draft letter that indicates what you need, or can talk with a staff aide who will do the actual writing. Identify each person to be contacted. Decide how the contact should be made and by whom. Set due dates, and set up a master file. Stay on top of the collection process, and do follow-up.

Exhibit 16 presents an example of a section on support and endorsement. The text alone is presented. Assume that the letters referred to are in the appendix as described.

EXHIBIT 16
Example of Section on Support and Endorsement

Example 4: Writing Skills for Retention of Graduate Students

SUPPORT AND ENDORSEMENT

The most significant support for the project comes from the president of ____ College. Dr. ____ has made it clear that retention will be a major focus of the college for the next several years. Dr. ____ has indicated in a letter to the proposed project director, Professor ____, that he not only endorses the project but will approve reduction in the usual share the college gets in indirect costs to make the project cost-efficient. He will support the allocation of faculty members for the project, and once the program has been installed, he will seek state funding for a full-time faculty line to keep the work as a permanent part of the academic program. President ____'s letter is presented in Appendix __.

Evidence of cooperation from all the directors of the graduate programs in Health and Human Services also appears in Appendix __. The directors have indicated that they will personally monitor their faculty, including adjuncts, to ensure that writing

continued

will become a part of the grading standards and that all faculty members will be referring students to the three levels of writing help.

The student representatives to the ____ College senate have also indicated support for the project. A letter from them, signed by the school's two representatives, indicates that there is widespread support for the project among graduate students. The letter is presented in Appendix __.

The chairperson of the Senate Committee on the Graduate Curriculum indicates that this project is being viewed with interest because of its implications for other graduate programs. As Professor ____ says in her letter,

> although I have always considered the concept of graduate-level remediation a contradiction in terms, the roundedness of the project and the inclusion of an intermediate writing course suggest to me that other programs could well benefit from a demonstration project. It has become apparent to me that, if our undergraduates are to have careers, they must have access to graduate education. And undergraduate writing is not always adequate to provide successful access. (See Appendix __.)

16

Future Funding

BEING FREE OF THE NEED FOR FUTURE FUNDING

Somewhere late in the narrative, probably just before the budget section, you will need to discuss what you expect to do after the project comes to an end. If you are discussing a two- or three-year proposal, you mention that, but it is the period after the whole project is over that is the subject under discussion. The funding agency wants to be convinced that you will not be on its doorstep for too long. Sometimes it will require progressively decreasing amounts of financial help in multiyear projects. Primarily, however, your future financial independence will come about in one or more of the following ways:

1. If your project has a successful run, your own institution is committed to incorporating the activity into its regular operations. This is called "institutionalizing" the project. It is a recognition of the significance of the idea. This may come about because
   a. The project represents a cost-saving innovation and, if successful, will pay for itself out of regular operating funds.
   b. Plans have been made to charge for the service or pass the costs along under reimbursement procedures, or to subsidize through some other means that incorporates the project into the regular operating budget.
2. Once this phase is completed, another funding agency stands ready to take up the next phase, because it is interested in seeing the program implemented.
   a. This can be a natural constituency, such as an employer group or major corporation funding an educational innovation, a

community group funding an effort that supports its population group, or a community foundation that supports local initiatives. It can be a private benefactor.

b. It can be a state or local governmental agency that has an interest in seeing the results perpetuated, such as a department of health supporting professional education in the health field.

c. It can be a foundation interested in the next phase or ready to support an extension to a new population group or new way of delivering the service.

3. The project may be a one-shot, self-limiting undertaking that will not need repeating or continuation once it is completed.

WRITING THE SECTION ON FUTURE FUNDING

The section should begin with an indication of the situation you will be in at the end of the first year of funding (and at the end of the proposed project period, if a multiyear project). You then need to substantiate your statement.

For example, if your agency or another agency or funding source will be taking over or funding future operations, explain that in the narrative, and send the reader to an appendix that documents the commitment. Remember that an appendix is not read unless the reader is told about it in the narrative. The letter(s) in the Appendix should spell out the exact nature of the future funding commitment.

If your agency plans to charge for the service or in some other way incorporate the activity into operations, document that a realistic analysis of supply, demand, revenues, and costs has been carried out.

If new equipment or facilities are to be funded by the present proposal, be sure to show how you will pay for staffing, maintenance, and/or new supply requirements.

If this is a one-shot funding situation, explain.

The section on future funding need not be long, but unless your project is a one-shot, self-limiting undertaking, a good deal of time may be needed to work out and document the actual future arrangements. To do this section effectively, meet with people in your agency to work out the plan and to decide how to go about getting the commitments in writing. Identify the sources, plan the calculations, draft the letters of intent or other documents needed, and decide which people to contact. Assign the right person to collect what you need. Set due dates; set up a master file. Stay on top of the collection process; do a follow-up.

Exhibit 17 presents two examples of sections on future funding, but without the Appendix material.

EXHIBIT 17
Examples of Section on Future Funding

Example 2: Ambulance Staff Training in Emergency Medical Services

FUTURE FUNDING

This proposal is for a one-year period, after which the training of paramedics in the administration of streptokinase in the field will be incorporated into the regular training that all new paramedics undergo at ____ Medical Center. A letter from ____, the administrative director of the hospital, to the director of prehospital care, in Appendix __, indicates that, assuming the success of the demonstration, future training costs will be absorbed into the annual operational and continuing medical education budgets of the Prehospital Care Department.

Example 3: City Children Involved in the Arts Community

FUTURE FUNDING

The program outlined in this one-year project, if successful, will be considered for incorporation into the curriculum of the city's public school system. A letter from ____, President of the Board of Education, indicates that if the demonstration is a success, "we are prepared to go before the Budget Department to have 10 percent of the allocations for extramural activities earmarked to support the involvement of artists of the ____ arts community in workshop sessions with students in the city system." See Appendix __.

The ____ Foundation has pledged the money to cover artists' salaries for a second year of operations, in the form of a "bridge grant," until arrangements are made to reimburse the artists through the city payroll. See Appendix __.

17

The Budget

OVERVIEW

One thing all grant and contract applications have in common is that they require a *budget* for the period being funded. The budget is an estimate of the expected future costs of delivering the work and products covered by the project proposal for a given period. It is broken down by expense categories. The budget is determined by the needs of the project and the limits set by the funding agency on the total amount and the expense categories for which it is willing to pay.

A multiyear proposal is generally asked to provide a separate budget for each year. Preapplications usually present a summary budget; final proposals are expected to provide detailed as well as summary budgets.

The budget tells the funder whether you know what you are doing. The budget will be examined to see if it is large enough to cover the activities the proposal promises to deliver, but it is also examined to see if it is padded to buy the institution things it wants that are not related to the project. The clarity of the budget says how much you can translate your proposal into real events over time.

Every budget item must be accounted for somewhere in the text. Every expense-generating activity mentioned in the text must be reflected in the budget.

The form of the budget and the names of the categories, as well as the amount of detailed breakdown under broad categories, can be set by the funding agency. If there is no form specified by the funding agency, the one presented here is a good one to use.

The budget section in a proposal usually includes three parts: the budget summary (for a Federal grant or some foundations, on the forms provided by the agency); a detailed budget, often on the forms provided, but sometimes presented by you at the end of the narrative; and a budget justification, part of the narrative preceding or following the budget, explaining all items presented in the budget that are not self-explanatory. It includes descriptions of the formulas, calculations, or assumptions upon which the budget figures are based, as well as explanations of the proposed expenditures.

PREPARATION

Only someone intimately involved with the project can write the budget, because it is intimately tied to the project activities. Read the instructions for presenting your budget supplied by the funding agency, and try to match the funder's categories with the guidelines presented in this chapter. This will help you make sure you understand the language used by the funder. If there is anything you do not understand, be sure to call the agency. Establish a working relationship with someone there. It is OK to ask for help. Budget errors are a sure way to court rejection.

Another important step is to make contact with the fiscal officer in your own agency. This person will have been handling grant budgets for others on staff, will know how to handle rates for special categories, and will know about such things as whether your agency has a negotiated fringe benefits rate, negotiated indirect cost rates, or an agreement on matching funds. You are not generally expected to do all this alone, but it pays to learn enough from such a colleague to do it yourself if you have to.

A helpful step is to lay out your plan of work for each month, as described in Chapter 13, and translate it into personnel and other costs. Go over every word of the text to make sure no activity or staffing need is left out. If an activity will take place in a period smaller than a month, note the number of days. For personnel, list the number required in each full-time title. For part-time staff, list the percentage of full-time. Remember to include staff members only for the months they will actually be working on the project.

CATEGORIES AND RULES

This section presents a detailed budget outline in Table 17.1, a description of the budget categories in the table, synonyms for category names, and some general rules.

TABLE 17.1
Example of Detailed Budget Outline

Table _. Title of Project, Year ending: Mo. , day, year (one page for each year)

BUDGET CATEGORY	First Year Estimates		
	CATEGORY TOTAL	GRANTEE CONTRIBUTION	REQUESTED

DIRECT COSTS

I. PERSONNEL COSTS

    Salary and Wages
        Professional Staff
        Support Staff
        Hourly Personnel
    Fringe Benefits
        Professional Staff
        Support Staff
        Hourly Personnel
    Consultants
    Contractual Services

    TOTAL PERSONNEL COSTS:

II. NONPERSONNEL COSTS

    Space Costs
    Rental, Lease, Purchase of Equipment
    Consumable Supplies
    Travel
        Local
        Domestic
        Foreign
    Communications
    Other Nonpersonnel Costs

    TOTAL NONPERSONNEL COSTS

TOTAL DIRECT COSTS

INDIRECT COSTS

TOTAL COSTS

GRANTEE CONTRIBUTION AS A PERCENT OF TOTAL COSTS: %

Heading

Every budget should begin with a table name that identifies what it is (See Table 17.1.) There should be a separate table for each year, or at least separate columns. There should be a separate column for the total needed for the year, the amount to be contributed by the applicant agency (the dollar values, whether the contribution is in cash or in kind), and as the last column, the amount being requested from the granting agency.

Direct Costs

The largest category is Direct Costs. It covers all the costs that will be attributable to the project, that is, that would not be incurred without it.

Personnel Costs (personal costs; personnel services)

Personnel costs are all costs of services rendered by people, whether on payroll or consultants.

Salary and Wages (wages and salaries)

The section on salary and wages covers all labor costs that appear on the regular payroll. This excludes contract services and consultants, for whom you do not pay fringe benefits. For each position you show the annual rate and the percentage of that time to be devoted to the project, and then the dollar figure for the annual cost to the project. Provide for enough staff to cover vacations, holidays, and sick leave.

For anyone assigned to the project from the existing agency staff, you cannot artificially raise the salary. The salaries must be those normally paid by the institution. Each person gets his or her regular salary from the institution, and the institution is reimbursed for that time. The only supplementary income possible is for a faculty member who is paid for a nine-month year but works during the summer. Such compensation is given a separate line in the budget. Salaries for newly created positions must be in line with those prevailing in the area for similar work and qualifications. It is best if you can place the new positions in the institution's already existing set of titles and salary schedules.

If you have the time, it is good to calculate labor costs by title, according to a formula by which you convert your needs to the labor hours needed each week or month, by title. The number of work hours in a day, times the number of work days in each month, less sick leave and vacation time, gives a figure for effective labor hours. This reflects actual time for working. If you divide the monthly labor hours needed by the effective labor hours, you have a figure for the number of full-time people needed per month in the given title. This can be used to incorporate part-time people into the calculations. Most budget projections are more crude than this. Remember to build in annual salaries that reflect expected wage increases. For new positions, use the average rate per year. This allows some flexibility for hiring along the range for the position, depending on the candidate. Do not skimp on staffing.

Professional Staff (or titles of professional staff)

For top staff members such as director and other key professional personnel, list the titles, and the names of the individuals if you know them.

Support Staff (or the titles of support staff)

List the support staff separately according to payroll categories. Give the numbers in each category, the annual rate, the percentage of time, and the total.

Hourly Personnel (or the titles of part-time staff)

This may include individuals to be hired for specific periods of time for data collection, regular part-time clerical work, and trainees. Show the category, the number in the category, the hourly rate, the number of hours, and the total for the year.

Fringe Benefits (staff benefits; personnel benefits)

Compensation for employees paid for in addition to wages includes *mandated benefits,* such as workers' compensation, disability, unemployment insurance, and FICA (social security, which is voluntary in some nonprofits), and *voluntary benefits,* such as insurance (medical, dental, long-term disability, life, and retirement or pension plan). Sick leave, holidays, vacations, extended leave, emergency time off, and educational assistance are also fringe benefits.

Some institutions have an arrangement with the federal government to use a fringe-benefit rate, a certain percentage of wages, instead of an itemized list of benefits. Your fiscal officer will know. The *negotiated fringe benefit rate,* or *composite rate,* is desirable because it saves the endless calculations, especially since not all benefits apply to all staff members, and some apply only after a period of time on the job.

Staff members can be covered at different benefit rates depending on job title, so the different rate categories should be listed separately, by title corresponding to the rate. You do the calculation for each category under wages and salaries and present the totals by rate category.

New employees on a project are assigned the same fringe benefits as those already employed. A new agency must conform to local practices in similar agencies. If fringe benefits must be itemized, each must be presented separately within the detailed budget.

Consultants (sometimes grouped with contract services)

A consultant is a professional whose services are required for a specific purpose over a finite period of time. Consultants are paid on a per-diem basis, and this does not include fringe benefits. Consultant costs are shown by category, with the number of hours, purpose, and per diem rate.

The rate must be commensurate with the nature of the services and the rates paid by the institution for similar services. Excess consultant hours and high rates are regarded with suspicion by funders.

Contractual Services (contract services)

Contractual services are performed by independent organizations in lieu of in-house staff members, sometimes for reasons of efficiency. Security, food service, bookkeeping, billing, data processing, housekeeping, laundry, and auditing are examples. List each service, the rate per job or per period, and the number of units of time the service will be required.

Fees must be comparable to those paid by the institution for similar services.

Total Personnel Costs

Total personnel costs are the sum of all personnel category costs.

Nonpersonnel Costs

Other than personnel costs (OTPS) cover all direct costs other than those for services rendered by people.

Space Costs (space and renovation of space)

Space costs are costs spent on the premises of the project that would not be incurred except for the existence of the project. If the project will be housed off the premises of the institution, rents, utilities, heating, and such items are included if allowed by the funder. If the project will be housed on the premises, only items such as renovation of space and floor covering can be claimed, and then only if the funding agency agrees beforehand. You would establish this through conversations with the agency staff. See indirect costs.

Prevailing rates for rentals per square foot and utilities should be stated and applied to the square footage and average monthly utility needs.

Rental, Lease, Purchase of Equipment (office and project equipment and furniture; permanent equipment)

Equipment and furnishings with an expected life beyond the period of the project are included; they are usually priced at over $500 per unit. Each such item must be listed separately, with the need for large or unusual items clearly explained in the budget justification. For items over $1,000, specific advance approval should be obtained. Current local prices should be estimated; evidence of competitive bidding will probably be required after grant approval. Some funding agencies do not approve any purchases of equipment, and some federal agencies require purchase through the Government Services Agency (GSA). Leasing has the advantage of automatic replacement in case of theft; purchase leaves the item with the grantee after the project is over. But since it is technically all the federal funder's property, you may find the agency claiming its property for use in another project. If listing rental or lease, specify the period and the rate per period.

Consumable Supplies (expendable supplies, equipment; office supplies, equipment)

Supplies, equipment, and furnishings expected to be used up during the period of the project are called *consumables*. The items are usually those priced under $500 per unit, even if large numbers of such items are to be purchased. Office supplies need not be itemized separately, but items unique to the project should be listed separately and explained. Current local prices should be estimated. Office supplies at so much per staff member (such as $150 to $200 per year), times the number on staff, can serve for your estimate. Include your calculations formula in the budget justification.

Travel

Travel is one of the most difficult categories for approval. Provide budget justification and details for each category that you need.

Local travel pays costs incurred for any given day beyond one trip to work and one trip home. So if a field team reports to the office first and then goes out to the site, and then goes home, each would be entitled to only one fare for that day.

Domestic travel is reimbursed on a per-diem basis, plus economy transportation for approved trips for selected staff members and consultants. Be judicious. Your institution's prevailing per-diem rate is usually accepted.

Foreign travel is almost never approved. You must have a very good reason.

Communications

New telephone installation, monthly estimates for telephone use, and sometimes postage are estimated under communications. Be careful not to overdo the phone-to-staff ratio.

Other Nonpersonnel Costs

Printing, publication, computer use, data processing, library acquisitions, special conference costs, and items that do not fit other categories are put into the category of other nonpersonnel costs and separately listed and explained.

Total Nonpersonnel Costs

Total nonpersonnel costs are the sum of all nonpersonnel costs.

Total Direct Costs

Total direct costs are the sum of personnel and nonpersonnel costs.

Indirect Costs (overhead costs; administrative and on-site space costs)

The costs of housing a project on premises and the costs of administrative services cannot be considered direct costs, because they are part of the overall operating costs of the institution and are not separately identifiable, or would be incurred anyway. They are called indirect costs. An agency may have a *negotiated indirect cost rate,* usually negotiated with the Department of Health and Human Services (HHS). This rate is calculated as an on-site or on-campus rate for an in-house project; it is calculated as an off-site or off-campus rate when the project is housed elsewhere.

The off-site rate is lower, but you also charge for space costs. When your agency claims a negotiated on-site rate, it can only claim renovation of space under space costs. (Space costs are direct costs.) When it claims a negotiated off-site rate, it can only claim space costs that are identifiable as direct costs for the project. The negotiated rates are charged as a percentage of wages and salaries or of direct costs less equipment, or by some similar formula. If you have such a rate it will often be accepted by an agency other than HHS.

Without a negotiated rate you are dealing with *overhead costs.* It is hard to find an agency willing to reimburse for overhead. You might be able to charge as "administrative and space costs" those indirect costs that can be prorated and charged to your project. What is listed under direct costs cannot also be billed under indirect costs.

Grantee Contributions (institutional contribution; cost sharing; donations)

Granting agencies like to see the applicant agency sharing in the costs of the undertaking, because this demonstrates commitment and responsibility. Some agencies actually require a cost-sharing arrangement or recommend that a minimum percentage of total costs be contributed. If you are asked to request decreasing levels of funding in a multiyear budget, you will probably accomplish this by progressively increasing grantee contributions as a percentage of total costs.

If you have grantee contributions you should have a column for them, so that figures can be entered for every budget category to which they apply. Sometimes a contribution, such as supplying the office furniture for a project, is overlooked. When such contributions in kind are listed, you estimate and list their dollar value. The articles and services become the property, theoretically, of the granting agency, so consider what you are donating. Professional staff time may be partly reimbursable and partly a contribution. When wages are a grantee contribution, they can also generate donated fringe benefits and indirect costs and thus have a salutary effect in raising the total contributed share. *Volunteers'* time can be priced and listed as consultant grantee contributions. But remember, you are responsible for delivering all the services promised, and you might then need a director of volunteer services.

Indirect costs are an excellent grantee contribution, since the project itself doesn't ever get to spend these dollars, even if granted. They go to the grantee's central office. On the other hand, institutions have come to rely on such funds for regular operating expenses. However, some institutions will pare down the negotiated indirect rate for certain funding agencies so that a proposal can be competitive in the race for grants. Calculate a contributed indirect cost figure using the same rate and formula as for requested indirect costs; you use the relevant totals of contributed budget items.

Total Costs

Total costs are direct costs plus indirect costs for each column.

Grantee Contribution as a Percentage of Total Costs

This is the percentage contributed by the applicant.

BUDGET JUSTIFICATION AND OTHER CONSIDERATIONS

The budget narrative follows the order of the budget categories. You write a description of each major expenditure category, unless the budget table includes the clarification. Use the same language as in the budget tables.

Remember to include an inflationary factor in your budget estimates. You are representing prices at least a year and more into the future. With collective bargaining agreements, future salaries are often known several years ahead. It is common to state in the narrative what your inflation figure is (usually the expected rate of price increases based on trend) and the categories to which it has been applied.

The Budget Summary

The budget summary usually includes subtotals for salary and wages, fringe benefits, consultants and contract services, space costs, rental lease-purchase of equipment, consumables, travel, communications, other costs, and indirect costs, plus the subtotals for personnel and nonpersonnel costs, direct costs, indirect costs, total costs, and grantee contributions.

Writing the Budget

Use copies of the budget forms obtained from the funding agency you are addressing to design the budget for the time period you have selected. You should have a Budget Summary, a Detailed Budget, and a Budget Justification for each year. You can append a salary schedule to support the personnel section. Give priority to funding agency budget categories and instructions. If no detailed budget forms are provided, follow the form presented in Table 17.1.

Use professional standards for appearance and layout. Use table titles. Be sure that everything in the budget is accounted for in the description of the project. Make sure that everything in the narrative is accounted for in the budget.

Note

Once the budget is approved and the project is on stream, most agencies will allow a certain flexibility in how you spend in each category. That is, if you keep "real time" records of your expenditures, you may find that you are drawing down the budgeted funds in some categories and spending less than expected in others. Many agencies allow a certain percentage over or under major budget categories without your having to get permission for such reallocations. Over a certain amount, you would need permission from the funding agency, and there are procedures for that once you are funded. It is a good idea to keep up to date in your records so you can apply for needed budget modifications well ahead of actual overruns. Note that such adjustments do not increase the total. Agencies are beginning to offer grantees more latitude in these areas without the need for prior consent.

Any attempt to obtain funds beyond those allocated in your grant or contract are tantamount to a new proposal. More likely to be approved is an extension of time if the project is running behind schedule and some funds are still unexpended.

Exhibit 18 presents an example of a project budget covering the first year.

EXHIBIT 18
Example of Project Budget

BUDGET

Detailed Budget and Justification

The summary budget is presented on the application forms called for, one page for each of the three project years requested. The table presents the detailed budget for each of the project years.

First Year

Personnel costs cover the project director at 25 percent release time, the administrative director at 15 percent release time, one equivalent full-time faculty member for the writing classes and tutorial workshops, a graduate assistant, and consultants.

The *project director* is a full-time full professor. The project is charged for her release time for nine months and at an hourly rate for the two weeks in the summer that she will be doing project work.

The faculty line for the classes and writing tutorials is calculated as the equivalent of a full-time *assistant professor*, midscale. The line is charged at 100 percent of time.

The *associate dean* is charged as a grantee contribution at 15 percent of 9 months of her annual rate.

The hourly rate for the *graduate assistant*, who will be assisting in the data collection, field tests, and administering of test instruments, is the one current for graduate assistants.

Fringe benefits are a negotiated rate (see attached letter of Agreement in Appendix __.) The current rate is 25 percent for payroll staff and 27 percent for release-time faculty.

Consultant time is being donated by professors ____ and ____ of the faculty, and the rate ascribed to grantee contributions is the midscale hourly rate for full professors.

Rental, lease, and purchase of equipment covers office furniture for the new faculty member, the writing tutorial files and desks, and use of duplicating equipment, all of which are being supplied by the applicant agency.

Consumable supplies covers supplies for duplication of materials, office supplies, postage, and instructional materials.

Communications covers use of a telephone, also a grantee contribution.

continued

Indirect costs are being charged at 8 percent of total direct costs. This is a special rate for educational programs. The current negotiated on-campus rate is now 61.9 percent of total direct costs, less equipment.

The *grantee contribution* is 17 percent of total costs.

Table _. Graduate Writing Skills Project: Budget for First Year, 4/1/89-3/31/90

FIRST YEAR BUDGET CATEGORY	CATEGORY TOTAL	GRANTEE CONTRIBUTION	REQUESTED
DIRECT COSTS			
PERSONNEL COSTS			
Salary and Wages			
Professional Staff			
1. Prof. _____, Project Director @ $65,302: 25% release time for 9 months;	$ 16,326		$ 16,326
Aug.: at summer rate of $60.58 pr hr.: 90 hrs.	5,452		5,452
2. Dr. _____, Administrative Director @ $65,534: 15% release time for 9 months.	9,830	$ 9,830	
3. One full-time assistant professor for 3 writing courses @ 3 credits; average of 13 hours writing tutorials per week, plus coordinating: 26 weeks	35,763		35,763
Hourly Staff			
4. One graduate assistant @ $10 phr. for 160 hours for field testing and data collection	1,600		1,600
Fringe Benefits for			
Release time Staff @ 27%	7,062	2,654	4,408
Payroll staff @ 25%	10,704		10,704
5. Consultants			
Faculty of Writing Center/ Eng. Dept. on curriculum & faculty workshops @ $58.72 phr. for 15 hours	881	881	
TOTAL PERSONNEL COSTS:	$ 87,618	$ 13,365	$ 74,253
NONPERSONNEL COSTS			
Rental, Lease, Purchase of Equipment	2,000	2,000	
Consumable Supplies	2,000		2,000
Communications	1,000	500	500
TOTAL NONPERSONNEL COSTS	$ 5,000	$ 2,500	$ 2,500
TOTAL DIRECT COSTS	$ 92,618	$ 15,865	$ 76,753
INDIRECT COSTS @ 8% direct	$ 7,409	$ 1,269	$ 6,140
TOTAL COSTS	$ 100,027	$ 17,134	$ 82,893

GRANTEE CONTRIBUTION AS A PERCENT OF TOTAL COSTS: 17.1 %

Note: The table presented here covers the first year only.

18

Letter of Transmittal, Summary, and Other Parts

Some sections of the grant proposal cannot be written until you have completed all the major sections presented in this book so far. The letter of transmittal or a form cover sheet, or both, the summary, a table of contents, an introduction, and a set of appendixes are such sections. These are discussed in this chapter.

LETTER OF TRANSMITTAL

A cover letter or letter of transmittal is not usually required for formal federal applications, but some do ask for a letter of transmittal along with a form cover sheet. Letters of transmittal, therefore, are essential for submissions to foundations, corporations, and some government agencies.

The letter of transmittal or a cover form tells the person screening the mail where to send the proposal for review; in a federal grant program there may be as many as 15 separate grant-making divisions and subprograms. The contents of the letter must stand alone, and you should never refer to it in any part of the document you are submitting. It must be self-contained, because it is often torn off and used separately.

You write the letter of transmittal after you have finished a draft of the narrative; you then know what to highlight. Be sure that any changes you have made during earlier drafts are reflected and that your information is up to date.

The letter of transmittal is also written to attract that first reader. Make sure it is addressed to the right person. The letter must be on the stationery of and signed by the highest-level administrator in your agency capable of committing the agency to a binding agreement. Generally, the grant writer proposes a rough draft for such a person to edit and sign. The letter of transmittal should cover the following:

1. To what section of the grants program the document is addressed, such as the number or letter identifying the section of the funding program to which you are responding and the name of the special section or program.

2. What response you are seeking. This may be a request to have an interview before applying; the document may be a concept paper. You may be requesting a response from the agency in the form of early critical feedback, with a hope of being invited to apply. You may be presenting a preapplication. Or you may be submitting the final proposal.

3. The time period for funding being requested.

4. The main activity: what the project will do and the type of program.

5. The population to be served, or "target population," with its location, numbers and characteristics.

6. The agency applying for funds (your agency name, type, function, location) and how it qualifies.

7. The total amount required and the amount requested for each year, unless there are special budget forms.

When a government form serves instead of a letter of transmittal, it must be signed by a chief fiscal officer. There is usually a place to check whether the document is a preapplication and places to enter the requested funds, agency information, the name of the person to be in charge of the project, and a box in which to insert a very brief abstract.

Remember that the letter of transmittal or the cover form should be signed by your chief officer *before* you run off the multiple copies of the document that are often called for. Examples of letters of transmittal appear in Exhibit 19.

EXHIBIT 19
Examples of Letters of Transmittal

Example 2: Ambulance Staff Training in Emergency Medical Services

LETTERHEAD STATIONERY OF GRANTEE AGENCY
PERSONAL STATIONERY OF CHIEF FISCAL OR EXECUTIVE OFFICER

NAME AND TITLE OF CORRECT   DATE
CONTACT PERSON AT FUNDING
AGENCY
CORRECT NAME AND ADDRESS OF
FUNDING AGENCY   RE: PROGRAM TO WHICH
       YOU ARE RESPONDING

Dear ____:

Enclosed is a concept paper that outlines the main features of a project to be undertaken by the ____ Hospital Center in ____ City. Based on prior phone contact with you, we are following your suggestion that we submit an early description of the proposal, enabling you to tell us whether your agency is a likely place to pursue funding. We appreciate the opportunity to have your critical feedback.

The Division of Cardiology, Prehospital Care Department, plans to submit a demonstration grant request under the demonstration section of your program in ____, XYZ No. __, Special Projects in Emergency Medical Care.

The one-year demonstration project would be organized to show that in-field, prehospital administration by paramedics of streptokinase will reduce the time now required to administer the drug to patients suffering a heart attack, and thus improve outcomes, without an increase in the incidence of adverse effects associated with administration of the medication in the hospital.

Funds are requested to train 37 paramedics and their in-house physician supervisors to run in-field streptokinase service. The proposed project would be for one year, hopefully beginning in ____ 19_. Out of a total cost of $____, $____ has already been raised to cover the costs of the equipment. $____ is requested to cover release-time training costs and evaluation; the hospital will therefore be providing a 40 percent grantee contribution.

The director of the project will be Dr. ____, director of the Division of Cardiology. His number is ____. Dr. ____ would be delighted to have the opportunity to discuss the project with you and have your critical comments. We would be very glad of the encouragement to submit a final proposal.

Sincerely yours,

Chief Executive or Fiscal Officer
Grantee Organization

continued

172

Example 3: City Children Involved in the Arts Community

LETTERHEAD STATIONERY OF GRANTEE AGENCY
PERSONAL STATIONERY OF CHIEF FISCAL OR EXECUTIVE OFFICER

NAME AND TITLE OF CORRECT   DATE
CONTACT PERSON AT FUNDING
AGENCY
CORRECT NAME AND ADDRESS OF
FUNDING AGENCY   RE: PROGRAM TO WHICH
                                       YOU ARE RESPONDING

Dear ____:

Enclosed, please find an application for a project grant in the area of Arts and the Community, one of the ____ Foundation's stated interests. The project being proposed is designed to bridge the gap between the resident arts community in ____ City and the students in public schools who rarely have contact with the art world, making for impoverished cultural life and mutual isolation.

The ____ Cooperative Center for the Arts and Education is a nonprofit, tax-exempt organization established as a cooperative agency in the ____ arts community. The cen-ter was organized ten years ago to promote audiences for the several arts it represents and to provide a vehicle for joint purchasing and cultural exchange with the community.

The proposed pilot project will be run by the center in cooperation with the public elementary school system. The ten cooperating units comprise three artists, two photographers, two sculptors, two dance companies, and a theater troupe. Each will offer two-hour open sessions once a week for 14 weeks, in the fall and spring terms of the school year, to groups of 15 to 20 students in the first through eighth grades, taken from the schools located in the central and poverty areas of the city. About 1,000 students, primarily from inner-city schools, will be served during the project year. The sessions will be work-in-progress, rehearsal, and thinking-out-loud work sessions in which the artists explore with the students what they are trying to achieve and how they are going about it. Once each term the students will attend finished performances or shows.

The requested funding for one year is $____. Contributions in kind will cover equipment and supplies in the amount of $____. Total budget: $____.

The director of the project is ____. She can be reached by telephone at ____, should there be any questions about the design of the project.

continued

EXHIBIT 19, continued

We look forward with anticipation to a favorable review by your board of directors and staff; the member artists are excited about doing the project.

Sincerely yours,

Chief Executive or Fiscal Officer
Grantee Organization

SUMMARY OF THE PROPOSAL

The summary, or abstract, is usually required for preapplications and applications. It is a section that must stand alone. It will probably be used alone in announcements of agency activity and for other internal matters. It may be torn off the body of the proposal.

You write the summary as if that is all a reader will see. And, when you write the narrative, do not assume that the reader has seen the summary. This means that, for you, there will be some redundancy. Don't worry about that.

The summary is usually only one page; sometimes two are allowed. Never write two when one is called for. The summary should have one short paragraph for every major heading, such as problem, objectives, methods, evaluation, support; sometimes it should include the requested funding. It should always include the time period and name the applicant agency.

The summary is also written after the body of the proposal so you can see what to summarize. Make sure the main features you think make the project attractive show up in the summary. Exhibit 20 presents examples of summary sections.

EXHIBIT 20
Examples of Summary Sections

Example 2: Ambulance Staff Training in Emergency Medical Services

SUMMARY: PROVIDING STREPTOKINASE THERAPY IN
PREHOSPITAL CARE

A demonstration project will show that in-field prehospital administration by paramedics of streptokinase, a clot-dissolving medication, will significantly reduce the time now required to get the drug to patients suffering a heart attack and thus improve outcomes, without an increase in the incidence of adverse effects associated with in-hospital administration of the medication.

The offerer is the Cardiology Division, Prehospital Care Department of the ____ Hospital Center in ____ City, a nonprofit, voluntary acute-care hospital that has been involved in the research in streptokinase.

Major activities are development of procedural guidelines for paramedics to follow in the field with potential recipients of streptokinase, covering indications, contraindications, and administration protocols; design of the content of paramedic training; training of the in-house supervisory physicians; actual training of 37 full- and part-time paramedics in six three-hour sessions over three weeks; and collection and analysis of patient and trainee data for evaluation purposes.

Objectives include successful training of the paramedics; reduction of the mean time required to administer streptokinase from initial encounter with the paramedics to the start of an intravenous (IV) infusion, currently at 90 minutes in an emergency room, to less than 60 minutes with IV in the field; demonstration of a correlation between reduction of time and reduction of mortality/morbidity; and demonstration that adverse affects associated with administration in the field are no more than the 5 percent now experienced in-house.

Funding for a one-year project is expected to require $____, of which 40 percent is a grantee contribution; $____ is requested.

Example 4: Writing Skills for Retention of Graduate Students

Title	GRADUATE WRITING FOR ACCESS AND RETENTION IN HIGHER EDUCATION
Abstract	A demonstration project will show that provision of basic and intermediary writing courses and remedial tutorial writing workshops for graduate applicants and matriculants in health and human services masters programs will result in increases in admissions and greater retention of students (largely those from minority groups or with English as a second language), who are now being turned away or failing because of poor writing skills.
Sponsor	Graduate Program in Health and Human Services Administration, School of Health and Human Services, ____ College. The school's graduate programs serve nontraditional working students, many of whom have

continued

EXHIBIT 20, continued

	English as a second language or have had disadvantaged educational experiences.
Problems	Minority individuals and those with English as a second language are sometimes held back from entry into the higher levels of professional functioning in health and human services because they are ill equipped to enter or stay in graduate school due to inadequate writing skills. Though their skills were sufficient to graduate with a baccalaureate degree, they are not adequate for graduate work and the professions for which the students are preparing.
Objectives	There will be increases in admissions and retention for those screened as writing deficient who take the courses/tutorials; students will show satisfaction with the program; faculty members will be using writing standards in grading and referring for writing help.
Methods	Thirty students per year in two sections of a basic graduate writing course; 15 a year in an intermediary writing course; and 66 students per semester receiving personal tutorial attention in sessions available through sign-up and faculty referral from 4 to 8 P.M., four days per week, during the semester; training of the cooperating graduate programs' faculty in incorporating writing standards in grading and referral to the three types of help; institution of an award for good writing; development of a writing test to screen applicants for admission and students with low grade-point averages; use of the basic course as a prerequisite for writing-deficient nonmatriculated students and counseling and referral for matriculants with similarly low averages.
Evaluation	Data will show 80 percent increases in admissions and retention among participants. Writing goals will be reached; the writing test will be successfully field tested; student evaluations will show satisfaction with the program.
Period	Three-year period commencing ____.
Request	$____ first year; $____ second year; $____ third year; total, $____. Grantee contribution will average ____ percent of total costs for each year.

TABLE OF CONTENTS OF THE PROPOSAL

The rule of thumb for the table of contents is to have one if the text is over ten pages. If you do include one, remember to list the appendixes and tables.

INTRODUCTION TO THE PROPOSAL

In Chapter 5 the introduction was presented as an option for people who like to write it early in the process. Now is the time to look at that first introduction again, to see if it still does the job you want it to do. Is it an interesting lead-in, and is it still accurate? Make any changes now that are necessary. The introduction should cover

1. The nature of what follows (discussion paper, preapplication, final proposal).
2. The specific part of the funder's offering you are addressing.
3. The time period for funding.
4. The total amount required and the amount requested (unless there is a formal budget form required elsewhere).
5. The main activity; what the project will do. The type of program.
6. The population to be served, or "target population," and its location, numbers, and characteristics.
7. The agency applying for funds (your agency name, type, function, location) and how it qualifies.
8. Special background material if appropriate.

Examples of proposal introductions appear in Exhibit 6, Chapter 5.

APPENDIX TO THE PROPOSAL

The appendixes are places to present materials that would impede the flow of the narrative but are important for your presentation. They are also a way to get space to present material when the proposal limits you to very few pages. Limitations on pages do not include appendix material, although some agencies limit the appended material too.

The most important thing to remember about an appendix is that the point it makes must be presented in the text. You send the reader to the appendix for more details. An appendix will not be read if you don't mention it in the text; it won't be useful unless explained in the text.

You should have a separate appendix for each type of material; the appendixes can be lettered or numbered, and could be separately paged and titled. If you have a table of contents, each appendix should appear. The types of material for which you might include an appendix are

1. Data such as tables to support points in the problem and methods sections.
2. Letters of endorsement and support.

3. Letters of agreement if there will be collaboration with another organization or plans for future takeover of the program.

4. Questionnaires to be used.

5. Curriculum outlines.

6. Special protocols.

7. Curricula vitae or resumes of proposed staff members and consultants.

8. An annotated bibliography.

9. Material demonstrating your agency's past successes.

10. Financial reports of your agency and tax-exempt status documents.

11. Documents of compliance with required organizational functioning such as

    The Civil Rights Act of 1964
    Affirmative action
    Protection of human subjects/informed consent
    Protection of animal subjects.

19

The Preapplication

OVERVIEW

When a funding agency uses a two-step application procedure, the first step is often referred to as a *preapplication* or *preliminary proposal*. Even if it is not the first formal step in applying for funds, most grant writers prefer a chance to have an early review of a preliminary proposal and may request such an early reading.

Many people believe that doing a preliminary proposal saves the extra work needed for the final proposal in the event of a refusal at the first step. In fact, you need just as much work to write a convincing preapplication, even if the actual document is shorter than the final application. The ones to do less work are the reviewers, who have fewer pages to read per proposal at the preliminary stage. The applicant actually benefits at the time of the final proposal's writing, since now most of the work has been done and it is a matter of filling out sections and revising to suit the feedback.

It is the feedback that comes from review of a preliminary proposal that makes it so attractive. The applicant is entitled (in a formal preapplication phase) to information on the reviewers' scoring and comments and the staff's reactions. Sometimes your follow-up phone call can result in detailed advice on how to revise.

WRITING THE PREAPPLICATION/ PRELIMINARY PROPOSAL

In writing the preliminary proposal, the first thing to remember is to work with the instructions for the preapplication, not those for the final application. They are often different in only a few significant ways, one of which is length.

Make a note early of the special requirements, such as single or double spacing, margins, type of paper, special formats for summary sections, and number of copies that must be submitted. Often, a call to your contact at the granting agency will be able to tell you whether the page limit is enforced strictly or whether you can go over by a page. Sometimes there are limits on the amount of appendix material. The contact person can tell you what would be appropriate and what unnecessary for appendix material.

Be sure to reread the funding agency's instructions before you submit. Even the most experienced writer will misremember what the page allowances are, whether a summary is needed for the preapplication, or what the appendixes can contain. Be sure to keep within the guidelines, especially for the number of pages allowed.

If you are asked to present a budget summary without a detailed budget, you will still have to prepare a detailed budget for yourself, so as to be able to deal intelligently with questions and reach realistic totals. You will probably need it to get approval at your own agency.

If no mention of evaluation is made in the preliminary proposal outline, put something in anyway; this shows a sense of responsibility. You can include it with the objectives statements, or under methods.

If you are applying to a foundation, be sure it is clear that the document is a preliminary proposal, for which you are requesting preliminary feedback. Final proposals are usually fairly short for foundations, and a preliminary proposal can be mistaken for a final proposal. Specify whether you are asking for a meeting or for a response, and note who has suggested that you write the preliminary proposal. You don't want to be reviewed by the grantor prematurely.

When you write the preliminary proposal, you should draw on the work you have already done, assuming that you have been writing the sections covered in this book. Make sure that there are no discrepancies in sections resulting from changes made in one section and not carried through in others. A good example is the need to refine your objectives after you do the evaluation section, or your methods section after doing the plan of work. It is easy to forget to follow through in the summary, introduction, objectives, or methods sections.

The same applies to the budget; any change in staffing lines or supplies will have repercussions for most of the totals and derived figures. Always check your columns down and then across before the final draft.

Hold yourself to the page limitations given by the funding agency. If none are given, 13 to 15 pages is a good limit to set. Sometimes an agency calls for only five pages: a concept paper. Page counts usually exclude the letter of transmittal, references, appendix materials, and summary.

Since you have already written your proposal sections in draft form, your job is to shorten for the preapplication and still keep the content. A wit once said, "I'm sorry that what I've written is so long. It would have been shorter if I'd had more time." It takes time to squeeze the vague or redundant phrase, the unnecessary qualifier, the hedging introduction from your writing, but it can be done with practice. As an example, the following paragraph comes from Exhibit 11, which has sample sections on significance:

> The impact of the program goes beyond the students themselves. It will allow them to enter graduate programs that will advance them professionally. The programs involved are in the social services and health, including occupations in short supply of effectively trained individuals, such as nursing, allied health services administration, social service workers, urban planners, and professionals in environmental control. These vital occupations stand to gain as more individuals with less than optimal educational preparation learn to write well enough to obtain graduate degrees. The jobs that they will fill will be steps on career ladders, and therefore attractive to the new arrivals. This can only enhance the quality of job performance and job stability in these occupations.

There is expendable language here. For a five-page preapplication, this can be reduced to read as follows:

> The project will make it possible for more graduates to enter the market in occupations that are in short supply. The fields of allied health and human services stand to gain as more people with less than optimal educational preparation learn to write well enough to complete graduate preparation. The professional jobs they fill will be steps on career ladders and will be attractive to the new arrivals. This can only enhance the quality of job performance and job stability in these professions.

Review the style notes in the appendix to this book. In addition, remember to write to your anticipated audience: intelligent professionals who may or may not be familiar with your particular field of interest. Make life easy for the reader. Be liberal with subheadings; repeat objectives under methods and evaluation so the reader will know what you are talking about. Don't use jargon; define your technical terms; and do not throw a bunch of abbreviations or acronyms at the reader, such as for your agency's name. Don't assume that the reader knows about your city, area, or agency. Remember, writing is an act of giving. Be generous to the reader.

Allow yourself enough time to get editorial feedback from the major collaborators with whom you have been working. If you have a fiscal officer, allow time for that person to check your budget. Allow time for the person who will sign off to provide feedback. Your final revision should be seen and approved before you actually submit. Then get your chief executive officer's signature *before* you run off the number of copies you are supposed to submit.

CRITERIA

For the federal government, the preapplication is really a first step to the final proposal: you are competing with others to be invited back. A major reason for rejecting applications is that the proposed project does not match the interests of the funding agency or misreads the agency's offering. Be sure to discuss in an appropriate place how the project fits the funding agency's interests.

Another major reason for rejection is the written quality of the proposal. Vague language, bare generalities without documentation, incoherent presentation, incomprehensible sentence structure, or lack of concrete details about what you are offering to do will defeat even the best idea. The proposal is no better than the way it is understood by the reader.

Proposals are also turned down for lack of evidence that the offerer has the capabilities to carry out the proposal. However untrue, if the document does not make a strong case for your staff's abilities, your facilities, and the agency's commitment, you will not be invited back.

There are other major reasons for rejection that have to do with the project itself. If the problem is not judged by the funding agency to be sufficiently significant, or if the approach is not considered by the funder to be sufficiently innovative or of poor design, you will be turned down. When the agency provides a list of review criteria, make sure the narrative has addressed them all; it would be foolhardy to ignore them.

RESPONSE TO THE PRELIMINARY PROPOSAL

The response from the funding agency can take several forms. This section briefly notes seven possibilities and appropriate actions on your part. For each, be sure you know the next step; verify it by sending a letter to confirm.

1. *You may hear nothing.* Check to be sure the document was received. Call or write to check on its status after a reasonable period — certainly before the date promised for decisions. But don't be belligerent.

2. *You may receive a request for further information.* Supply everything needed as soon as possible.

3. *You may receive a request for a site visit.* This is not a good or bad sign. The funder is seriously interested, but wants to clear up some points personally. Ask ahead of time what to expect, the number of persons coming, who on your staff the site team expects to see, whether they would like a tour of your facilities, and so on. Note whether you are to be host or whether the team must supply its own food. Prepare your staff beforehand by going over the weak points in your proposal and developing a common approach. Make sure everyone involved at your institution knows about the visit. If you ignore people or departments they cease to be your allies. Have local supporters available if appropriate. On the day of the visit, be sure the staff functions normally but is prepared for a sudden summons to meet. Have a comfortable place to meet; refreshments but no "favors." Be natural, prepared, enthusiastic, and calm.

4. *You may receive a request for a meeting at the funder's office.* This may be what you asked for. Be prepared with project details and the rationale for the project. Know the weak points and be able to defend them; practice dealing with hard questions. Bring your top people, but only if they are familiar with all the project details. Have one major spokesperson. At the meeting, listen carefully to see whether the funding people really understand the proposed project. Clear up misunderstandings tactfully, but effectively. Be sure the funding agency people see the tie with their agency's goals. You may describe how your agency came to develop the project.

5. *You may receive suggestions for changes,* in writing, by phone, at a meeting, or during a site visit. Consider the legitimacy of the request, whether the integrity of the project is affected, whether you are able to comply. Can parts of your project be omitted without damaging the vision and effectiveness? Find out the consequences if you do not

comply. Do not make snap decisions; avoid deciding on the spot. Once you decide against making the required changes, find another funding source. If you do decide to make changes, follow their consequences throughout the document, including the budget, evaluation, due dates, and plan of work.

6. *You may be turned down.* You generally have a right to know the reasons for rejection, and federal agencies provide a mechanism for this that includes the right to see the reviewers' comments and to be told staff comments if relevant. If you are rejected without being given the reasons, or if invited to, call or write to receive the reviewers' comments and the reactions of the agency staff. Was the rejection a result of a misunderstanding of the project? See if you can clarify and be reconsidered or if there is anything else you can do to be reconsidered. Don't back agency people into a corner or insist that they take the blame for a misunderstanding. Provide a way out. Get suggestions on what you can do to improve your chances.

It is a little-known fact that some government agencies will let you submit a final proposal even if you were turned down for the preapplication. Talk with your contact person on the funding agency staff about this possibility. If you believe that your project was misunderstood or that you didn't get a chance to properly present your project in the limited space allowed, by all means submit a final proposal; but be sure to get the reviewers' and the staff's comments, so you will know what needs clarification or elaboration.

Find out if the rejection is due to lack of funds; if so, ask when to apply again.

If the rejection was due to the inappropriateness of the funding agency for your type of program, ask which agency is recommended.

If you are encouraged to resubmit, find out if you can use the name of the individual who suggested this. Never use the name without permission.

7. *You may be told to go ahead and submit the final proposal.* Great! But also go back for reviewers' and staff's comments. This will help you prepare a better final proposal. If your preapplication is approved and if intergovernmental and/or HSA review is required, use the preapplication text as a notification of intent. Then proceed with the final funding proposal.

20

The Final Proposal and Beyond

Here you are!

IF THERE WAS A PREAPPLICATION

If you have received comments on a preapplication that cause you to amend your project in any way, you need to work through the consequences throughout the document. The best places to start are the two schematic layouts you drew up for the basic components and the evaluation design. Next, follow through in the plan of work. The plan of work and the layouts help you to see the ramifications of the changes, and they become a guide to revision. Then, do not forget the consequences for the budget.

Budget changes from the time of the preapplication to the final proposal are welcome if they result in reductions; any increases must be kept to a minimum unless you have been asked to add a component. The funding agency will view the preapplication budget pretty much as a commitment.

WRITING THE FINAL PROPOSAL

Prepare your final proposal according to the requirements of the agency's application forms and any intergovernmental review requirements. It will now include a detailed budget, curriculum vitae for staff and consultants, an evaluation design, a section on organizational capability, and most of the other topics covered in this book that may have been omitted from the preapplication. For foundations, the final application will be relatively short.

Using copies of the actual forms required by the funding agency, prepare the actual proposal, including any support materials. This should bring together the work you have already done so far. Now you have the opportunity to revise and tighten your material; the bulk of the work has already been done.

Include, in the appropriate order and under the appropriate names used by the agency, the material covering the topics listed in the outline below. If the agency presents a less detailed outline or no outline, you will benefit by including material on all of the subjects presented. Note that only the chapter references for the topics are given, because every item has already been covered in the text. Whenever you think you have a strong point, make the point. Take nothing for granted. Make sure the narrative flows. Be sure you have adequately addressed each agency criterion.

Make sure you have time to submit well before the deadline. One to three months ahead allows time for answering questions and for HSA and intergovernmental review.

Arrange for the proper signature on the application or letter of transmittal, and make the number of copies required by the funder.

OUTLINE FOR FINAL PROPOSAL

1. Letter of Transmittal. See Chapter 18.
2. Summary. See Chapter 18.
3. Introduction. See Chapters 5 and 18.
4. Need and/or Problem Statement. See Chapter 6.
5. Objectives. See Chapter 7.
6. Project Description (Methods). See Chapter 8.
7. Significance of Methods. See Chapters 8 and 10.
8. Evaluation Design. See Chapters 11 and 12.
9. Significance of Impact, Anticipated Results. See Chapter 10.
10. Sponsorship, Organizational Capability. See Chapter 14.
11. Support and Endorsement. See Chapter 15.
12. Future Funding. See Chapter 16.
13. Plan of Work. See Chapter 13. (Can also go after evaluation.)
14. Budget, Including Justifications. See Chapter 17.
15. Appendix Materials Mentioned in Text. See Chapter 18.

THE CONTINUING PROCESS

If you will be involved regularly in grant writing, you should consider the process a continuous one. Maintain folders on organizational endorsements and successes. Keep a file on funding agencies and their policies. Keep up relationships with the funding people you have begun to know.

Learn who the likely funding sources for your agency are, and cultivate a line of communication with them. Keep up with the state of the art and professional literature. Keep alert to the types of projects that can advance the needs of your clients or the discipline.

Prepare descriptive material about your agency that can serve most proposals. Get on the mailing lists of relevant funding agencies, especially the request-for-proposal lists of federal agencies.

And good luck!

Appendix: On Style

STYLE TIPS

1. Read all forms and instructions provided by the potential funding agency and then follow them carefully. Plan a format to fit your proposal and the forms you must use.

2. There may be an apparent lack of logic in some application forms. They may appear to ask for the same information several times or request details in a sequence other than the one you would choose, or may use language differently from your usage. Try to follow the instructions as closely as possible regardless of these reactions on your part. You may want to use your synonyms as part of your topic headings to help you keep the logical flow.

3. Make sure that your written presentation of the problem, objectives, and method is stated in terms of the target population and that it is clear and interesting and makes a compelling case.

4. Maintain a balance between conciseness and enough detail to give the reader a clear idea of the project. Examine the guidelines and speak to others funded by the particular agency to determine what the agency's preference is in striking such a balance.

5. Explain technical phrases and words unless they are commonly used and easily understood. Avoid jargon. Assume that the reviewers are intelligent, but give them the courtesy of enabling them to understand what you say without recourse to additional sources, a dictionary, or a glossary. Similarly, don't use many abbreviations or acronyms that make the reader go back to check in order to recognize, and *always* present the term or name followed by its acronym or abbreviation in parentheses the first time you use it, and again in each major section.

6.   Write as though the proposal may get only a quick review. Have the eye guided to the key points by use of headings, subheadings, underlined key phrases, indented lists, and spacing. Omit needless introductory phrases. Use active rather than passive verbs. Be precise.

7.   Write in such a way that you cannot be misunderstood.

8.   Be sure that the narrative flows smoothly and logically from one section and paragraph to another. If it helps the flow, use bridges to tell the reader what you are writing about.

9.   For visual effect avoid long, unbroken paragraphs. Space between paragraphs; use generous margins. Double-space unless told to do otherwise.

10.   Footnotes and literature review may be needed to show that you know the field, but the amount of documentation and detail called for is less than for a term paper. Always put quotes in quotation marks, and give citations for paraphrases as well as direct quotes. Select a style of referencing and footnoting and stay with it consistently.

With one footnote style you can put the author's name, a date, and a page number in parentheses in the text; you number and list the references alphabetically by author in the back. The text might look like this: text text (author's name, p. 2). If you will be citing the same author for more than one document, you would include the date, as follows: text text (author's name, year, p. 2). The date of publication clarifies which reference you mean, and the page number tells the reader where to find the item to which you refer.

Another way is to simply put a footnote number in the text after your quote or paraphrase, beginning with [1] for the first reference. Each footnote gets the next sequential number, even if the document has been cited before. The page cited is shown in the footnote and not in the text. The citations are often gathered at the end, in numerical order; they are then called notes, or references. The citations are called footnotes only if they appear at the bottom of the page on which they occur.

Still a third way is to list your sources at the end, in alphabetical order by name, and numbered. You then cite the number of the reference within parentheses in the text, with the page number if you are making a specific citation. As an example: text text (3). The number 3 refers to a reference document with that number, and the number appears each time you cite the reference. A factual reference would look like this: (3, p. 14).

Notice that footnote numbers in the text are superscripts, [3], and numbered citations in the text are in parentheses, (3). Don't confuse these. Also remember that it is more flowing to write "as pointed out by *name,* text text text, footnote or citation number, text text" than to make your point and give a footnote or citation number with no acknowledgement that you are making a citation.

Collected notes or references follow the narrative and precede any appendixes. A *bibliography,* which can be presented as an appendix, is different from collected references. It includes sources that you may not be citing. A bibliography is put in alphabetical order by author. Every reference cited should also appear in the bibliography.

Textual comments (little comments addressed to the reader) can be done with an asterisk in the text and the comment with its asterisk at the bottom of the page. Numbered notes would be gathered at the end of the text.

11.   Put space-consuming drawings, charts, tables, and all resumes, vitae, letters, and similar support materials in appendixes unless otherwise indicated by the instructions. Place short tables and figures in the text as soon as they are mentioned or on the page following the first mention. Never present a table or figure without telling the reader what you are pointing out and what is being presented. And be sure the table or figure is understandable in and of itself, numbered in order of presentation, and sourced.

For material such as tables and letters to be placed in appendixes, remember the following: Always present the key points in the text so that the reader does not need to refer to the appendix. Always make the appendix self-sufficient so that it can be fully understood without the text to explain it. This means that tables must have descriptive titles, including the dates to which the data refer. Column and row headings should be easy to understand. And every table must have an ending that presents the source(s) of the data. For footnotes in a table other than source notes, use superscript letters.

It is sometimes useful to give each appendix a letter and to number its pages with the letter. For example: A-1, A-2, etc. With the appendixes separately numbered, there can be no misunderstanding about the length of your narrative. If an appendix has a large number of items, such as letters of support, it can have a cover sheet listing its contents. Every item in an appendix must have a title.

12.   Check that the pages are numbered, in order, and that copies are complete. Use consistent numbering and format. Be sure the text has been checked for spelling, grammar, and typos and that the copies are clean and clear. Before the proposal is submitted, make sure all the required information has been included.

SELF-EVALUATION CRITERIA
FOR PROPOSALS

1. Is there a logical sequence? Can a reader follow the sequences?
2. Are any questions left dangling?
3. Are the terms used understandable?
4. Is everything called for in the instructions included?
5. Was a convincing case made?
6. Does the writer seem to know what he or she is doing?
7. Does the program seem worth doing?
8. Does this read as a professionally competent job?
9. Is the writer motivated?
10. Does it read as though the writer would do a good job?
11. Do you feel you gave your best to this?
12. Did you avoid facing problems you know exist?
13. Did you collaborate with the right people for information, approval, support, or feedback?
14. Did you avoid dealing with opposition or different points of view from other professionals, staff, or administrators?
15. Did you avoid sections that were called for, hoping the omissions would not be noticed?
16. Did you take shortcuts you are not happy with?
17. How do you feel about the program now? About your chances of being funded? Does it show?
18. Are you ready to submit the document?

NOTES ON FORMAT

1. You cannot begin a sentence with a number. You must use a word. *42 arrived.* (incorrect) *Forty-two arrived.* (correct) *Those arriving numbered 42.* (correct)

2. Never leave the last or first line of a paragraph alone on the top or bottom of a page of text.

3. The left-hand margin should be greater than or equal to the right-hand margin. The top margin should be greater than or equal to the bottom margin. No margin should be under 3/4 inch.

4. When you double space and have short paragraphs, indenting for paragraphs creates a confusing layout. The same is true for numbered lists. It is easier, more attractive and modern to use block formation, with extra spaces between paragraphs. Single spacing within lists is fine. Some printers used with word processors cannot intermix single and double spacing. In such a case, use 1.5 spacing unless the funding agency really cares about having everything double spaced. (Publishers have other rules.)

5. The following style for headings is useful:

Title: FULL CAPS

Major headings: FULL CAPS UNDERLINED

Subheadings: Upper and Lower Case Underlined

DRAFTS

Expect to go through several drafts. For the first one, say everything you would like to get down. For the second, try to edit so as to eliminate unnecessary phrases and improve the logical sequence. Then present a copy and the funding agency's instructions to someone who knows the field, and another set to someone who has a good use of language but doesn't know the field. Have each one comment on the logic, clarity, tone, and persuasiveness and watch for questions that seem unanswered or sections that are unclear. Ask for comments on the idea and method.

Read the draft again yourself and edit freely. Submit to all those who must approve, and ask for editorial suggestions. Accept the ones that make sense. Always edit to clarify any section that is unclear or has been misunderstood.

Selected Bibliography

This is a selected bibliography touching on the major sources available to help the grant writer. Directories are listed by title; no date is given for publications that are updated periodically. The reader is recommended to the latest available edition in each case.

DIRECTORIES

Activists' Guide to Religious Funders. Center for Third World Organizing, 3861 Martin Luther King, Jr. Way, Oakland, CA 94609.

America's Newest Foundations. The Taft Group, Washington, DC 20016.

Annual Register of Grant Support. National Register Publishing Co., Macmillan Directory Division, Wilmette, IL 60091-9978.

Catalog of Federal Domestic Assistance. Executive Office of the President, Office of Management and Budget. Superintendent of Documents, Government Printing Office, Washington, DC 20402.

CFAE Corporate Handbook of Aid-to-Education Programs. Council for Aid to Education, 680 Fifth Ave., New York, NY 10019

Complete Grants Sourcebook for Higher Education. David G. Bauer, ed. New York: American Council on Education/Macmillan.

COMSEARCH Grant Guides. The Foundation Center, New York, NY 10003, 212 620-4230.

Corporate 500: The Directory of Corporate Philanthropy. Public Management Institute, San Francisco, CA 94107.

Corporate Foundation Profiles. The Foundation Center, New York, NY 10003, 212 620-4230.

Corporate Fund Raising Directory. The Taft Group, Washington, DC 20016.

Corporate Giving Yellow Pages. The Taft Group, Washington, DC 20016.

Directory of Building and Equipment Grants. Research Grant Guides, Dept. 3B, P.O. Box 4970, Margate, FL 33063.

Directory of Financial Aids for Minorities. The Grantsmanship Center/Reference Service Press, Redwood City, CA 94065.

Directory of Financial Aids for Women. The Grantsmanship Center/Reference Service Press, Redwood City, CA 94065.

Directory of International Corporate Giving in America. The Taft Group, Washington, DC 20016.

Foundation Directory and *Supplement.* The Foundation Center, New York, NY 10003. 212 620-4230.

Foundation Grants to Individuals. The Foundation Center, New York, NY 10003. 212 620-4230.

Foundation Grants Index Annual Edition. The Foundation Center, New York, NY 10003. 212 620-4230.

Foundation Guide for Religious Grant Seekers. Scholars Press, P.O. Box 6525, Ithaca, NY 14851.

Foundation IRS 990-PF Returns. The Foundation Center, New York, NY 10003. 212 620-4230.

Fund Raiser's Guide to Capital Grants. The Taft Group, Washington, D.C. 20016.

Fund Raiser's Guide to Human Service Funding. The Taft Group, Washington, D.C. 20016.

Fund Raiser's Guide to Private Fortunes. The Taft Group, Washington, DC 20016.

Fund Raiser's Guide to Religious Philanthropy. The Taft Group, Washington, DC 20016.

Guide to Corporate Giving. American Council for the Arts, New York, NY 10018.

Handicapped Funding Directory. The Grantsmanship Center, Los Angeles, CA 90014.

National Data Book. The Foundation Center, New York, NY 10003. 212 620-4230.

National Directory of Corporate Charity. The Foundation Center, New York, NY 10003. 212 620-4230.

National Directory of Corporate Public Affairs. Columbia Books, Inc., 1350 New York Ave., N.W., Suite 207, Washington, DC 20005.

National Guide to Foundation Funding in Health. The Foundation Center, New York, NY 10003. 212 620-4230.

National Guide to Funding in Aging. The Foundation Center, New York, NY 10003. 212 620-4230.

Resource Guide to Church Funding Sources. Women's Technical Assistance Project, Center for Community Change, 1000 Wisconsin Ave., N.W., Washington DC 20007.

Source Book Profiles. The Foundation Center, New York, NY 10003. 212 620-4230.

Taft Corporate Giving Directory. The Taft Group, Washington, DC 20016.

Taft Foundation Reporter. The Taft Group, Washington, DC 20016.

REFERENCES

Commerce Business Daily. Superintendent of Documents, Government Printing Office, Washington, DC 20402.

Federal Grants & Contracts Weekly. Capitol Publications, Arlington, VA.

Federal Register. Superintendent of Documents, Government Printing Office, Washington, DC 20402.

Foundation Fundamentals: A Guide for Grantseekers. Patricia E. Read, ed. 1986. The Foundation Center, New York, NY 10003. 212 620-4230.

National Center for Health Services Research. *Small Grants Program in Health Services Research.* Public Health Service, DHHS, Rockville, MD 20857; NIH Guide Distribution Center, Bethesda, MD 20892.

Office of Management and Budget. *Administrative Circulars* FMC 74-4, A-21, A-102, A-110, A-111, etc. Government Printing Office, Washington, DC 20402.

United States Government Manual. Superintendent of Documents, Government Printing Office, Washington, DC 20402.

CLEARINGHOUSES/DIRECTORIES

The clearinghouses and directories listed are central sources of research and project reports on general or specific topic areas. They can be contacted directly, or you may consult a Federal Depository Library.

ETA Research Development and Evaluation Projects, U.S. Department of Labor, ETA/OSPPD 200 Constitution Ave., N.W., Room N 5639, Washington, DC 20210, 202 535-0677.

National Clearinghouse for Alcohol and Drug Information (NCADI), Box 2345, Rockville, MD 20852, 301 468-2600.

National Technical Information Service (NTIS), Department of Commerce, 5285 Port Royal Road, Springfield, VA 22161, 703 487-4600. NTIS is the central source for the public sale of U.S. government-sponsored research, development, and engineering reports, foreign technical reports, and reports on the work of other government agencies and grantees.

Resources in Education (RIE). Educational Resources Information Center (ERIC), Government Printing Office, Washington, DC 20402.

EVALUATION

The publications listed below all contain extensive further references for specific aspects of evaluation design and analysis.

Abt, Clark C. *The Evaluation of Social Programs.* Beverly Hills, Calif.: Sage, 1976.

Besag, Frank P., and Peter L. Besag. *Statistics for the Helping Professions.* Beverly Hills, Calif.: Sage, 1985.

Campbell, Donald T., and J. C. Stanley. *Experimental and Quasi-Experimental Designs for Research.* Chicago: Rand McNally, 1966.

Cook, Thomas D., and D. T. Campbell. *Quasi-Experimentation: Design and Analysis Issues for Field Settings.* Chicago: Rand McNally, 1979.

Edwards, Allen L. *Techniques of Attitude Scale Construction.* New York: Appleton-Century-Crofts, 1957.

Epstein, Irwin, and Tony Tripodi. *Research Techniques for Program Planning, Monitoring and Evaluation.* New York: Columbia University Press, 1977.

Fink, A., and J. Kosecoff. *An Evaluation Primer* and *Workbook.* Beverly Hills, Calif.: Sage, 1980.

Green, Lawrence W., and Frances M. Lewis. *Measurement and Evaluation in Health Education and Health Promotion.* Palo Alto, Calif.: Mayfield, 1986.

Kuzma, Jan W. *Basic Statistics for the Health Sciences.* Palo Alto, Calif.: Mayfield, 1984.

Miller, D. C. *Handbook of Research Design and Social Measurement.* New York: McKay, 1964.

Patton, Michael Q. *Qualitative Evaluation Methods.* Beverly Hills, Calif.: Sage, 1980.

Rossi, Peter H., et al. *Evaluation: A Systems Approach.* Beverly Hills, Calif.: Sage, 1982.

Thompson, M. S. *Benefit-Cost Analysis for Program Evaluation.* Beverly Hills, Calif.: Sage, 1980.

Windsor, Richard A., et al. *Evaluation of Health Promotion and Education Programs.* Palo Alto, Calif.: Mayfield, 1984.

Index

ABOUT THE AUTHOR

ELEANOR GILPATRICK is a professor at the Hunter College School of Health Sciences, City University of New York, where she is Director of the Master's Program in Allied Health Services Administration. Dr. Gilpatrick has extensive research and funding experience in the areas of human resources, job analysis, and career/curriculum development, particularly in the health field. At Hunter College she teaches a graduate course in program planning, funding, and evaluation.

In addition to many research reports written for various funding agencies, Dr. Gilpatrick has published widely in labor literature and is author of two previous books, *Structural Unemployment and Aggregate Demand* and *The Occupational Structure of New York City Municipal Hospitals* (Praeger, 1970), with Paul Corliss.

Dr. Gilpatrick holds a B.A. from Brooklyn College, an M.A. from the New School for Social Research, and a Ph.D. from Cornell University.